We live in a village world,
... we belong to a world community.

L. B. Pearson, et al.
Partners in Development,
Report of the Commission
of International Development

The world created by the Son.
The world God saved by the Son.
The world which is yours.

Heb. 1:2; I John 4:14; I Cor. 3:22

the politics of hope

BY ANDRÉ BIÉLER

Preface by
Dom Helder Camara

Translated by
Dennis Pardee

William B. Eerdmans Publishing Company

Library of Congress Cataloging in Publication Data

Biéler, André.
    The politics of hope.

    Translation of Une politique de l'espérance.
    Includes bibliographical references.
        1. Church and the world.   2. Church renewal.
3. Civilization, Modern—1950-   I. Title.
BR115.W6B4513   261.8'3   74-14980
ISBN 0-8028-1588-X

Translated from the French *Une politique de l'espérance*, © Éditions
Labor et Fides (Geneva) and Éditions du Centurion (Paris), 1970.

This book was prepared at the request of the Association of Evangelical Theological Seminaries of Brazil. The author dedicates it to these seminaries, and to the Institute of Philosophy of the Catholic University of Recife, as a token of gratitude for their warm welcome.

preface

In spite of our desire "to listen to what man says of himself today, to his own ideas about his calling and about his contemporaries, by examining the major events of our time," we would be swamped by mountains of documents, often mutually contradictory, if we did not make a judicious selection.

André Biéler, Professor of Theology at the universities of Geneva and Lausanne, has enormously facilitated our task by his decision to study "man's calling in today's global society" through the analysis of three major ecumenical texts[1] that to him "appear to have a profound understanding of man and which proceed by analyzing his situation as objectively and realistically as possible."

The author reminds us that "our use of these documents will not keep us—indeed the opposite is true—from constantly referring to the great theological traditions of the different confessions on which they are based, which they in fact carry forward and renew."

But the documents he has chosen "place us immediately at the heart of the human struggle, at the critical points of history as it unfolds, where our fellow-men are face to face with life's toughest realities and where the Church must ask itself some introspective and critical questions about the deeper meaning of its modern calling and about its basic motives for continuing an active presence in the world."

As his point of departure, Biéler adopts this axiom: "The truth about man and society can become known only through continual study of Christian revelation and by an ongoing examination of the historical reality of a constantly evolving world." From this axiom he deduces two conclusions: (1) "Truth is the product of debate, a debate between theologians, who have the calling (but not the monopoly) to search out and proclaim the presence, action and will of Christ for today's world and that of tomorrow, and specialists in every discipline of human knowledge. . . ." (2) "Considering on the one hand the permanent mystery inherent in the knowledge of the living Christ, and on the other the dynamic renewing power this same Christ communicates to man, to society and to the whole world, it is obvious that the knowledge of Christ's presence, his action and his will in the world can never be gained once and for all. There is always such a distance between Christ and his creation in perpetual movement that no Church can claim to describe what truth is without a constant renewing influx of power from Christ and his Holy Spirit, without the renewing force of historical realism."

The author of *The Economic and Social Thought of Calvin* then asks Rome, Beirut and Uppsala certain questions about "man's calling and the destiny of society"; about "alienated humanity and its restoration"; about "the church's mandate and its renewal"; about "temporary tragedy and temporary politics."

This book must be studied chapter by chapter with careful attention to each thought.

As regards man's calling, perhaps the key expression is "technological man, vicar of God."

And what he has written on the "first-fruits of a new world" is really beautiful and encouraging!

If Marxists could read objectively and without prejudice Biéler's comments on true alienation, they would realize a depth and breadth in this word that perhaps they have not yet sensed—a word they use so often in their slogans against religion in general and Christianity in particular.

The Church also has something to gain from meditating on its responsibilities in launching this new world, in providing a basis for development, in fostering social transformations; something to gain from meditating on its role as a proof of the unity of mankind, as a place where political consciousness can be formed, as a place of reconciliation, as a source of action in the world, as a critical conscience for society, as a bearer of the critical Gospel, as a sentinel for the peoples of the world. But it is indispensable for the Church to prepare itself for its critical role and, especially, to have the courage to recognize and confess its weak points: the racism of which it cannot always rid itself; its involvement in national, economic and ideological conflicts; its conservative laziness; lack of conscience—the great ecclesiastical sin; the noninvolvement of its lay members; its tendency to shortsighted parochialism; its deadly political and social conformity; its fear of change or uncritical docility in the face of change; its collusion in abetting social decline; its indifference toward real unity; its ecclesiastical egocentricity; its false realism and irresponsibility; its pious, frightened patter....

This presentation of three major ecumenical texts, strengthened by the lively manner in which they are presented —the secret of the book's success—brings us to the personal conclusion that, for the time being, the Church does not need new statements on social topics. But we must recognize that time is working against the Church. The young, especially, run the risk of thinking that the Church is tranquillizing itself and soothing its conscience by issuing beautiful statements full of nice words.

We should complete the work of the Ecumenical Conference on World Cooperation for Development by pushing for an Ecumenical Conference that would function as a movement of public opinion in favor of applying in practical terms the encyclical *Populorum progressio* and the conclusions of Beirut and Uppsala. We need an Ecumenical Conference that would not be afraid to perform a liberating function by fostering justice in the relations between the developed and developing portions of the world. As long as injustice exists on a global scale, no peace is possible in man's world.

Dom Helder Camara,
Archbishop of Olinda and Recife

contents

reconciliation of nations and of classes. A ceaseless combat
for unity among men. An unwearying battle for development.
A struggle in common with all men. In the Church and outside
the Church.

A. The Church, First Form of the New World   77

The Church, source of development. The Church, seedbed of
social transformation. The Church, first-fruits of human
catholicity. A specific catholicity. A pluralism respectful of
diversity. Catholicity realized in holiness. The Church, where
political awareness comes about. The Church, source of reconciliation. The Church is not a goal in itself. The Church, a
source of action in the world.

B. The Church, Critical Conscience of Society   86

The Church, bearer of the critical Gospel. The Church, sentinel
for humanity. The necessary criticism of powers. The Church
must prepare for its role as critic. More collaboration with the
outside. A continual revitalization from wthin.

C. Failure and Triumph of the New Humanity   89

1. The Churches' Necessary Confession of Guilt   90

Racism in the Church. The Church, accomplice of nationalistic,
economic and ideological conflicts. The conservative laziness
of the Church. The great sin of the Church: lack of conscience.
The abdication of the laity. An active minority would be sufficient. Shortsighted parochialism. A deadly political and social
conformity. Fear of change. Fear and irresponsibility provoke
violence. An uncritical docility to change. The ambiguity of
secular catholicity. The ambiguity of ecclesiastical power.
Complacency toward the rich and the powerful. Desertion in
conflict. Complicity in social backwardness. Indifference toward real unity. Acceptance of false forms of unity. Ecclesiastical egocentricity. Complicity in the arms race. False realism
and irresponsibility. Pious, frightened patter. Words with no
practical results.

2. The Church Renewed by the Grace of Discernment and the Courage of Repentance   101

The importance of simultaneous local and worldwide plans.
The collective responsibility of Christians for development and
disarmament. A call to an objectively motivated repentance.
Conversion: behavior and structures transformed for action.

3. The Persevering and Triumphal Church   105

A deferred triumph. A resolute advance. An immutable hope.
The triumph is certain, though presently only glimpsed. Cease-

less combat. Shared suffering. Persistence through tragedy. The time for anticipatory action. Only one criterion. Many signs, but often ambiguous.

The permanence of Easter and Good Friday. Good Friday: temporary. Easter: definitive. The time of temporary politics. Society on the march. The relative nature of every political project and choice. The eternal nature of every political project and choice. The time of ideologies and utopias. The desecration of ideologies. The need to save a part of ideology. The need to create realistic utopias. Political realism. The political ethics of Christians. The necessity for the Church to examine its politics. Where and how the Church may become politically involved. An arbitary distinction: temporal and spiritual. A proper pastoral discernment. Honest, unprejudiced dialog. The ambiguity of all Christian witnessing.

The primary necessity: a general realization of (a) the new possibilities, and (b) the gross inequalities. Create a common will to change. Create a will for better collaboration. A better division of the fruits of development. Developing countries. The developed countries. Revolution. Violence and non-violence. A united worldwide society. Beyond the national state. Regional unity. World integration. The Churches must show the example by bursting their national and confessional structures. A new education. From destructive national armies to a common world development. The necessary development of international law. A world government. The decisive international role of the Churches. The necessary mobilization of every parish. Once more: the Churches must be equipped.

An active hope. The dark pilgrim march. Where is the Church? The unstable situation of the faithful Church in any society. In palaces and slums. Truth first, not success. A tragic optimism.

introduction

How are we to go about describing man's calling, his place and his mission in modern global society?

Let us begin by listening to what man says of himself today. What are his own ideas about his calling? What conclusions does he draw about his contemporaries when he examines the major events of our time? His observations have been set down in innumerable documents. Thus we must choose those documents which have the profoundest understanding of man and which proceed on the basis of an analysis of his situation that is as objective and realistic as possible. That is why we have decided to examine three of the major ecumenical documents of our time. The first in chronological order, the papal encyclical *Populorum progressio*,[1] dates to 1967. The second is the most ecumenical document of our time. It was put together by qualified representatives from all Christian confessions, chosen from theologians and laymen of the non-Catholic denominations brought together by the World Council of Churches as well as from experts belonging to the Catholic Church. This document is the report of the Conference on World Cooperation for Development, held in Beirut, Lebanon, April 21-27, 1968.[2] The third is the report of the Fourth Assembly of the World Council of Churches, which met in Uppsala in July of 1968.[3-4]

Our use of these documents will not keep us — indeed the opposite is true—from constantly referring to the great theological traditions of the different confessions on which they are based, which they in fact carry forward and renew.

The involved Church   We have chosen to base our discussion on these three modern texts because they depict clearly for us the great human problems that summon Christians to new responsibilities. They place us immediately at the heart of the human struggle, at the critical points of history as it unfolds, at the nerve-centers where our fellow-men are face to face with

15

life's toughest realities and where the Church must ask itself some introspective and critical questions about the deeper meaning of its modern calling and about its basic motives for continuing an active presence in the world. The ecumenical nature of this existential research and of the documents that make it possible is everywhere evident in the reflections of Christians on today's burning problems. The influence of the major spiritual currents that went into the formation of modern Christianity, the Catholic, Orthodox, and Protestant traditions, may be observed in them. The Catholic tradition is most visible in the numerous references to man's nature troubled by sin, but not entirely defaced. The problem, from this perspective, is to find his true nature in the blurred image of modern man — by means of the gift of supernatural virtues given by Christ to ensure the perfection of this nature. Protestant theology, radicalized in the teaching of Karl Barth and Dietrich Bonhoeffer, does not consider itself capable of picking out man's true nature and his destiny in the human form we come to know by our own means — this image has been too deformed by sin. The only valid picture we can get of mortal man is that of the New Man who broke into history, Jesus of Nazareth. The incarnate, divine Word alone can give meaning and direction to all of creation. The Orthodox tradition tries to reconcile these two tendencies by living in permanent contemplation of Christ's resurrection. For this resurrection gives direction to all of creation, a conscience to all humanity, and a hope based on what it has already become and on what it is capable of becoming.

First-fruits of a theology of the future   In the documents we have chosen to guide our thinking, these three tendencies emerge and intertwine in kaleidoscopic fashion, largely as a result of the lively ecumenical dialog going on today throughout the world. This characteristic intermingling shows that the truth and active presence of Christ within his Church are partially attested by each of the confessional traditions, but Christ himself goes infinitely beyond these traditions and he communicates to the embattled members of his body a dynamic and creative force that no theology can completely account for. Rather we can discern in these texts, and in the traces they reveal of the three main ecclesiastical currents, the first-fruits of a more elaborate ecumenical theology that will go beyond parochial traditions to do justice to the complex and many-faceted reality of the living Church throughout the world.

Interdisciplinary ecumenism   There is today general agreement that the knowledge of reality concerning man and creation cannot be the exclusive domain of theologians. For the fulness of this truth is given both by Christ's revelation to man and by the dynamic, changing world that he created and is still mysteriously guiding through the vicissitudes of history toward its final destination. The truth about man and society can become known only through continual study of Christian revelation and by an ongoing examination of the historical reality of a constantly evolving world.[5] From this statement, which we will use as a basic axiom, two conclusions are formed: the first is that truth is the product of debate, a debate between theologians, who have the calling (but not the monopoly) to search out and proclaim the presence, action and will of Christ for today's world and that of tomorrow, and specialists in every discipline of human knowledge. These experts are non-ecclesiastical, and it is their duty, if they are Christians, to make an effort to understand how Christ's presence, action and will are expressed in their specific area, and how Christ's actions relate to all the other disciplines that study the mysteries of creation. The second conclusion is this: Considering on the one hand the permanent mystery inherent in the knowledge of the living Christ, and on the other the dynamic renewing power this same Christ communicated to man, to society and to the whole world, it is obvious that the knowledge of Christ's presence, action and will in the world can never be gained once and for all. There is always such a distance between Christ and his creation in perpetual movement that no Church can claim to describe what truth is without a constant renewing influx of power from Christ and his Holy Spirit, without the renewing force of historical realism. This is the basic reason, because we are Christians and in spite of our more or less direct attachment to a specific confession and our justifiable pride in the contributions made by that confession to ecumenical understanding, why we can gain so much from studying the theology of the confessions that make up the universal Church. For all the members who make up the invisible Christ, who are drawn together in him to form one body, have something essential to proclaim based on their particular understanding of this living Christ. But we must thereby accept that none of these theologies can be expected to give a complete and decisive account of the entire mystery of Christ. This is true, first, because Christ never lets himself be circumscribed by a theology and, second, because each theological system is part and parcel of a particular historical and cultural situation, and each is only one expression of the historical and geographical diversity the Lord disposed in order to make up the complementary diversity of his own body. Only his glorious advent can mark the end of man's multiplicity.

The precariousness of Church[6] structure   Today's major ecumenical documents and the assemblies and groups that drew them up, with the help of experts and specialists in the various areas, have pointed out with remarkable clarity two of the most typical characteristics of the global Church: its greatness and its misery. The misery first: faced with the tragic events that shake today's world and agitate its inhabitants to their very depths, the Church's response is only too human, only too indecisive. There is no doubt that it is surprised and at a loss, *as are all men,* to deal with events so vast and swift that it must make a decision before it has even had time to determine their dimensions and consequences. It is altogether proper that it should recognize its smallness and weakness faced with the tremendous issues at stake in today's events, for modesty is and must remain one of its primary virtues. Indeed, it shares its fundamental uncertainty as to the future of humanity with all men and with all this world's sages. For they also are surprised by the rapid changes taking place in the world — at least to the extent that the latter are even perceived. Only those high on ideology can afford to give the last word on man's destiny today and tomorrow. But contemporary ecumenism also shows the greatness of the Church. For, in spite of the improvising to which it is forced by the rapidity of every kind of historical and sociological change, it has been able to make clear statements on these changes, statements common to all the confessions of the world. When it accepts its condition of poverty, it can be the instrument of a truth that is not de-

pendent on the newness of events but which nonetheless comes
to it as it traverses these events.

Ecumenism on the front line   The universal church,[7] in the
person of its most responsible members, occupies a position on
the front line of the human conscience. The work of the Holy
Spirit within it — and only by faith does it have any guarantee
of possessing the Spirit — gives it a certain spiritual intuition,
shared by almost all denominations. This intuition enables it
to analyze events lucidly and to propose concerted action to
its members even though it is aware that its choices are subject to the last judgment and that the grounds of its arguments,
especially in the area of theology, are never fully assured. Is it
not true that the Church's greatest intuitions, often in contradiction to its own past and to a part of its members intent
on keeping hold on the past, were frequently a step ahead of
formal explanation, which itself was only worked out later by
theologians (although theologians may occasionally be involved in creating an innovation)? It is at such times that we
can see that the Church, prepared by the work of the Holy
Spirit, has received from its Lord the liberty it needs to confront the events of history in spite of the restraints — sometimes
safeguarding restraints — of the conservative forces that tend to
paralyze this liberty. In any case, no one can deny, when the
ecumenical documents and warnings of the Church of these
last decades are compared with the spoken and written statements that express the collective conscience of peoples and
governments, that the Church today is functioning as a clear-
sighted sentinel, free and even prophetical. One example will
suffice to illustrate this fact.

The encyclicals of John XXIII and Paul VI, the Second
Vatican Council and even more the ecumenical conference
"Church and Society," held in Geneva in 1966, drew the attention of the world to the danger for all humanity inherent in the
unequal development of the rich and poor nations, the increasingly inhuman nature of economic and technological
development within the rich nations over against the explosive
revolutionary situation that was the worldwide result of that
growing disparity. Now, it was not until 1967 that the developing countries recognized their situation in a concerted way and
came up with the "Charte d'Alger." There appeared in May

1968 the first symptoms, visible to every eye, of a worldwide revolutionary situation with epidemic potential that so many superficial observers had refused — and still refuse — to take into consideration.

We do not mean to say that Christians have been the only ones to understand these events. Far from it. But they were among the first, collectively, to give them serious consideration, to endeavor to discover their causes, to find remedies for them and to apply such remedies with effective resoluteness.

The hidden specificity of the Church   What makes the Church truly prophetic, however, is not that it speaks of the world's problems sooner or later than others. It is rather that it speaks at the proper time according to its own specific message. The conformity of silence and passivity could be just as harmful to its witness as the conformity of speech or action motivated purely by a desire to harmonize its voice with the world's. Now what characterizes modern ecumenical research to a great degree is its endeavor to base its judgment of contemporary events on the Gospel message. Its decisions are thus, to the extent that such a thing is possible, independent of modern ideologies.

Nevertheless, though the Church tackles concrete problems from its own perspective, it cannot avoid saying or doing what others do or say from other motives. And thus it cannot help being accused by outsiders of conforming to the pressure of one group of men or another, or of partially espousing one ideology or another. This is how it was for Christ. There was no real proof for nonbelievers, either in his speeches or in his acts, that he was not guided by human motives like everyone else or that he was the bearer of a specific divine message. His adversaries always assigned him to some well-defined social group. The specificity of his message was discovered only by those whose conviction came from their faith. The same ambiguity is ever veiling the Church's testimony, whatever religious, social or political form it may take. But the essential thing for Christians is to make an effort to line their lives up vigorously with their faith and to translate this faith into contemporary terminology.

The social backwardness of the Church   We must add, however, that although the promoters of the modern ecumenical movement form a clear-sighted vanguard for the world, it must be deplored that they are just that and only that within the historical Churches. Within these Churches they make up, along with a lucid minority of Church members, only a relatively small group when compared with the conforming, unthinking majority. The documents we are here examining are a long way, sad to say, from representing the voice of the common Christian conscience — at least as far as members are concerned. In fact, one of the major problems facing all Churches today is how to make their members come to grips with the upheavals of our time, with the changes that have taken place in mentalities and practices, and with the Christian's responsibilities toward these upheavals.

A worldwide social ethics   The goal of the following lines is to point out the importance of contemporary ecumenical thought for man's temporal and eternal destiny and for the future of the global society now taking shape.

Any program dealing with man's calling and destiny in today's society must include, alongside cultural, economic and political considerations, an examination of problems facing the couple and the family. Nonetheless, we will devote no special treatment here to those problems — not because they are of minor importance but because their great importance has led the various Christian Churches to dedicate a special measure of care to them. Innumerable theologians have devoted vast amounts of thought and ink to their resolution. This is true to such an extent that many believers and ministers feel that the thrust of Christian ethics reaches beyond the individual only as far as the couple and the family. Thus, up to the present, social, economic and political problems have gotten short shrift in theological and ecclesiastical thought. And since it is to the credit of modern ecumenical thinking to have re-entered this area of human life, too often neglected by Christians because it is too difficult, it has seemed to us important to put our primary emphasis on problems of this nature.

A difficult juncture   We have tried, moreover, to avoid an excessive emphasis on *concrete problems,* in favor of pointing up explicitly the *juncture* between concrete problems and the

Christian message. For this juncture is one of the main problems the modern ecumenical movement must surmount. It is a fact that many believers are completely helpless before their social and political responsibilities with all their spiritual and technical complexity. Without necessarily being indifferent or hostile to the practical recommendations given to them by their Churches, they are still a bit uneasy as to the spiritual justification behind these recommendations. They do not consider them to be explicit enough. And this lack of explicitness often serves as an alibi against any change in conduct — a change that requires courage and self-sacrifice. Others are surprised to see the sudden interest shown by the Churches in social problems they had previously neglected to a certain degree. These people try to provide a theological justification for the Church's abstention even though it is a relatively recent phenomenon in Church history.

Everywhere the social implications of Christian theology — itself in crisis because of the trend of current thinking — are at the center of theological thinking. Some, scandalized by the apparent indifference or reticence on the part of theologians and Churches toward the suffering world, conclude too hastily that any theology is intrinsically incapable of resolving man's greatest problems. They reject any explicit reference to the Gospel as a criterion for practical action. And furthermore they see their political involvement and their Christian faith as being totally identical. Others, disgusted by such confusion, retire to the ivory towers of an individualistic theology and a passive expectation of the Kingdom of Heaven. Such theology serves paradoxically as a spiritual justification for two mutually contradictory attitudes: abstention from any form of politics (since the world is in any case hateful and given over to devils), or unreserved political and ideological conformity that leaves the individual complete freedom to carry out a policy of personal interest (since politics as thus conceived has its own rules with no connection to the Kingdom of God).

But in fact these two attitudes, both based on the same theology, only justify and emphasize, by the reaction they provoke, the theological secularism they claim to combat. And in turn the theological orientation they choose is justified by the excesses of secularism. In order to avoid the sterile exaggerations and the useless struggle of these extreme positions, we must find the elusive middle of the road by a proper evaluation of social phenomena. The way is not easy because theological and ecclesiastical thinking have partially neglected it since the industrial revolution, either because of spiritual complaisance and laziness, or because the unconscious effect of certain tacit accommodations between religious groups and the dominant political powers was to abandon the middle of the road. In any society the privileged class tries to ensure that the Church does not threaten any of its privileges (political, economic or social).

First steps in research   It should perhaps be added, to conclude this introduction, that the following pages in no way claim to propose final solutions. They are only a part of that laborious and precarious research which we think constitutes one of the primary duties of today's Church as it advances down the unknown path of history with no surety other than the certainty of being led by the one and only Master. The Master gives enough signs of his presence to comfort the Church in its sufferings and to buttress its hope, but not enough to incite in it a proud claim to a knowledge of the present and the future that it does not possess.

Not claiming definitiveness, this book has even less claim to exhaustiveness. Its only goal is to pick out from contemporary ecumenical thinking a few of the major lines of reflection and to indicate some of their practical applications. Given the brevity of our four chapters, the vast subjects cannot appear in all their theoretical or practical vastness.

And, finally, must we say that the very choice of texts to be quoted and discussed is itself subjective and the examination they undergo is the result of personal interpretations? But is it not also true that every testimony rendered by the Church must be assimilated and to a certain degree retranslated by every believer before it can take on life? Our essay is an attempt at synthesis of certain texts that, be it said, do not lack contradictory aspects. Our idea was to emphasize what unifies them, while purposely leaving aside their contrary aspects, this being, in our opinion, of lesser importance.[8] We have no pretensions of presenting the only possible or the only proper interpretation.

the politics of hope

One: man's calling and the destiny of society

The Christian Churches have undertaken an analysis of the modern world. They have seen in the unfolding drama of contemporary history an exact reflection of what God has shown us in the Gospel. In it can be seen a humanity made up of beings endowed with exceptional qualities, capable of astonishing intellectual and physical performances. But they are also capable of fearful crimes, including the most odious subjection of their neighbors and the most extreme degradation of their own nature. What we must determine, then, is whether this human being is forever condemned to this ambiguity or whether his calling as a man summons him to another destiny. The ecumenical documents being examined here provide an answer to this question. They remind us first of all that, according to biblical teaching, man's destiny, although it is special, is nonetheless tied up with the destiny of all creation and God assigns to each of his creatures a precise life-course. So, before pursuing the study of man's calling, we must learn the destiny allotted to all of creation — the work of God to which man belongs. Then we will study the special calling God directs to mankind. This first chapter, then, treats the created world and men as God wants them to be. Here we will not yet be investigating the use, good or bad, that man makes of the life offered to him, or how he responds to his calling. Those questions will be taken up in the second chapter.

A. THE DESTINY OF CREATION

What is the goal intended for creation? Theologians have given ample reply to that question over the years. But on examining these responses we cannot avoid noticing that they were products of their time, in part based on perfectly authoritative biblical material, but reflecting the bias of the age. Moreover, they were based on a static view of the world, in harmony with a rural and artisan economy. The result was that for centuries men considered the world to be governed by a wise and all-powerful God who ensured the temporal conservation of creation, whereas this same God endeavored on another plane to summon man, his favorite creature, to an eternal destiny with no direct relation to secular history.

It was only on the level of this eternal spiritual experience that the drama of the fall was located which made necessary the rescue operation undertaken by the Son of God at the price of his death on the cross. But the salvation thus brought about affected only individuals, one by one, and only in their inner life. It only partially modified their temporal condition, which was said to be governed by the laws of nature alone, and which was imagined to be without any direct relation to eternal life. All social life and all politics were exclusively under the sway of a natural order of providence that God had organized for creation in order to assure its temporal survival. The new life of the soul afforded by the Holy Spirit was thought to make no fundamental change in man beyond his spiritual and eternal destiny. The created world, man's exterior life and societal elements unrelated to the Church received only, therefore, the benefit of a momentary survival. Inevitably evil finished by triumphing over them — which only justified their condemnation and their death in the end. The biblical references to a new creation were therefore generally considered applicable only to souls in a future world. And these souls did not seem destined to benefit in that after-life from a natural, biological setting in any way comparable to creation as we know it, in spite of the repeated references in the Creed to the resurrection of the body.

The riches of an open tradition   Tradition did contain many correctives for this schema, but most ecclesiastical circles paid little attention to them. The Renaissance and, even more, the eighteenth century were necessary to enable free thought and the acquisitions of the exact sciences to put the traditional schema to the test. It became more and more obvious that man was linked to the destiny of nature, and that nature, far from being static, had exhibited ever since its ancient origins a continual process of development in creation toward greater complexity and greater liberty. It was seen that man, the last stage in this process, had followed an analogous path, described by the developing sciences. He had been producing, during recent generations, increasingly complex societies and weaving a tighter and tighter web of social relationships. It was then preceived that the social environment determined more and more radically the temporal destiny of the individual, limiting his freedom at the same time that it provided him with new possibilities for expansion and externalization. The static world and the old conservative schema of social order were thus fundamentally confuted and the Church found itself forced to revise its conception of man and society.

Fortunately, the Church had preserved in its theological tradition, and even more in the treasure of biblical revelation that it had interpreted far too partially, many precious elements that enabled it to work out its new orientation.[1] The rediscoveries of modern ecumenical theology are often only a revaluation, in the new terms, of old thinking that has temporarily been overshadowed.

1. *From the Theology of World Conservation to a Theology of Human Development*

Biblical theology was formed either as a reaction to current conceptions considered to be contrary to divine revelation or, on the contrary, by borrowing language as well as cultural and religious aspects that were already in existence and then giving them new meaning. For many religions of the ancient Near East, as well as for numerous primitive religions still active today, God or the gods reveal themselves essentially through nature.

Deified nature   All of nature — fields, forests, mountains, the earth, water and fire — are held to be so many outer manifestations of the divine presence, now favorable, now harmful to man. The object, then, is to reconcile nature and the gods hidden in it by all expedients, all the while remaining subject to it. Religious man fears nature, is in awe of it, venerates it. He has no hold on it. Rather it is nature that seizes him.

The living God of history   But the God of Israel revealed himself in a different way. He did not make himself known first or foremost by means of nature. He appeared at the most important moments of the entire people's history, was revealed to the people by the great individuals of history. Moses made him known when the people of Israel were delivered from Egyptian bondage. God revealed himself by hiding, that is, he spoke to men, but refused to be given a name. He was at no man's mercy and men were summoned to obey him. He spoke to them by the events of history and these historical events attested, at least in certain circumstances, to his judgment and condemnation or on the contrary to his grace. Moreover, this God who was often hidden but who nonetheless broke into history, announced to Israel not only that he was the God of Israel, but that he was the God of all other nations. And all these nations are marching toward a single goal that is itself prepared by the history of Israel. All of history is included in the destiny of Israel; in Israel "all the families of the earth will be blessed."[2]

Nature subordinate to history   Nature is not foreign to this history. It is the vast setting in which man, created in the image of God, is supposed to carry out the Creator's purposes for his creation.[3] For Israel, the God of history is the same as the God of nature: both are governed by the same active will. And also, as a result of the *covenant* God established with the people of Israel, and through them with all the peoples of the earth, man is called to serve this God and to make manifest in the world the fulness of his Kingdom. Nature itself must serve him and bend to his purposes. The whole earth is full of his glory,[4] and its fertility — especially that of the promised land — expresses God's love for man, that same love on which the covenant was based. All of creation, all of nature is thus associated with the history of mankind. Its intended purpose is the same as man's: to make manifest the glory of God and to express the magnificence of his reign.[5]

The God of history and nature   The well-known accounts of creation were handed down to teach us that all nature is the scene and setting for human history[6] and that the creation of the entire universe is only an introductory phase to the history of humanity. The Lord of history and of this creation is complete master of the universe, which belongs to him and to which he has assigned a precise goal.[7]

Second Isaiah opens up an even more interesting vista: the creative work of God is the preliminary condition for his redemptive work, which was to be carried out down through man's history.[8]

The destination of history and nature   Thus, in the Old Testament, neither nature nor history is self-authenticating. Their purpose is provided for them by something beyond themselves. There will be a termination of this history, a final realization that will go beyond both nature and history in their actual forms. The vision of Old Testament theology goes beyond history, but the "beyond" is inseparable from what happens on this side. And even more important, the "beyond," the fulfilment, is what gives meaning to all of creation and to all of history, for it takes upon itself full participation in the present age and all that it comprises. Moreover, this fulfilment is already proclaimed and prefigured in man's present condition every time he meets God. It is this *meeting* between God and the human being he has created which is the heartbeat of all creation and which gives it meaning from beginning to end. Nature is also programmed according to this event. Nature is its setting, the place where it takes place and the necessary condition for its occurrence. But it is the meeting that gives meaning to nature. And however strong the destructive powers may be that contest this plan by attacking both nature and humanity (we will discuss this point in Chapter II), they are in the final analysis incapable of overthrowing it.

2. *Christ, Origin, Center and End of All Creation and History*

The New Testament gives the Old Testament proclamation in more precise terms. We knew from the Old Testament that there was a purpose for all creation and for all of history: that they have a beginning, a center and an end. The New Testament states that this meaning, this beginning, this center and this end are revealed to us by the eternal existence of the Son of God and by his historical incarnation as the Christ, Jesus of Nazareth. He is in himself the perfect fulfilment of the covenant by which God once proclaimed his love to the people of Israel, and through them to all nations. He is the explanation of past human history, but, more important, he is the prophetic revelation of man's future, triumphant history. He proclaims the final glory of human society by fulfilling it in advance, and gives the first sign of it in his own resurrection.

Adam and the new Adam   Not only is he at the beginning and at the end of human history, its alpha and omega, but he is just as surely the beginning and the end of creation where that history had its beginnings and where its fulfilment will be played out. In his divinity Christ is the author of history and creation.[9] But in his humanity he completes it and transcends it. The new Adam, according to Paul, is more than the old Adam restored. He is the crowning act of God, the New Man, not only created in God's image but the definitive and unsurpassable revelation of that image. Now we may know that first portrait, made a part of human history under Pontius Pilate, but its final form will be revealed in the new world proclaimed and inaugurated by his resurrection. It is in this New Man and in this new world that creation, nature and humanity find their destination and a vision of their fulfilment.

The extraordinary energy of history and creation   This vista reveals the tremendous energy inherent in the development of creation and history. And this energy corresponds perfectly to the external manifestations the natural and social sciences describe. Christ, therefore, is not only the spiritual restorer of a certain part of fallen humanity. He is also the conductor of humanity in its entirety, and he commands the course of its history in order to bring it to its final goal — a goal that has presently been only glimpsed at the time of resurrection.

The starting point for this grandiose enterprise may be seen in the two creation stories of Genesis. But the end-point does not consist of a simple restoration of fallen humanity. The end-point as described by Revelation 20 and 21 is much more than a replica of the Garden of Eden. Man is not pictured living there in a primitive state; rather he lives in a city, the very symbol of human culture. The old Adam was only a living soul; the new Adam is a life-giving spirit.[10] The outcome of creation and history is therefore the end of a process, the termination of a progression and, if you please, the end-point of progress, although this view of progress has nothing to do with the conceptions and representations of it so readily conjured up in modern progressist theories. So by taking into consideration all the essential biblical data on man's destiny and that of creation, by removing them from the various schemes in which conservative theology has too easily classed them, we can see that it is impossible to speak of a conservative, unmoving order of things for the unfolding of history. Rather we must think of a growth process, of development. And this is true even though we must recognize a marked discontinuity between the period of historical development and that of its final realization, even though the course of this historical development is always ambiguous due to contradictory factors, even though the process remains subordinate to the dominant mystery of history, that of election, of judgment, of grace and of God's sovereign liberty toward the world's destiny and toward the fate of each creature.

A specific process of growth   When endeavoring to understand this view of development, one must take into consideration its peculiar characteristics and its specific rhythm. It cannot be identified with any current notion of progress or development. But it does enable us to understand that there are harmonies and analogies between the objective data of the exact sciences and of scientific history (which can set down only the external phenomena of natural and human history), and the basic data of biblical revelation. Certain biblical texts refer to a destruction of the world after the last judgment; others claim that the new creation has already begun. We are thus led to believe that this destruction has already begun before the last days and, by the same token, that the renewing of creation has already begun in our historical period. It will reach completion at that very moment when what must be destroyed, both qualitatively and quantitatively, is destroyed. The judgment of God and the action of his grace have been simultaneously at work since the beginning. Good Friday and Easter are the proof.

Christ, the motivating factor in the development of creation
We may thus believe, fully conscious of being in agreement with biblical revelation, that it is Christ who animates the mysterious development of humanity and of the nature to which it belongs. Nature is both man's environment and his

biological sustenance. Christ is the motivating factor behind societal development toward an increasingly refined and well-integrated complexity that is a prefiguration of the harmonious interrelations between all members of the society to come. And he is the one who assures the outcome of their history, since he is their beginning, their end and their fulfilment. This growing complexity of creation, of which man is the most finely honed result, this growing complexity in the history of human societies in all their multitudinous and diverse manifestations, in no way reduces the fact of their unity. This is what the Churches proclaimed at Uppsala when they declared: "The Word of God testifies to the unity of creation, and to the unity of all men in Christ."[11]

B. THE FUTURE OF HUMANITY

The dynamic action of the Creator and Animator of the entire world, of nature and of history, must find its response in the participatory and creative work of man. To be a man means first of all answering this call to action, this call to voluntary and spontaneous collaboration with the Lord of all creation. The proof that man has recognized his own identity, has fulfilled his humanity, is his response to this call, a response that makes him a *responsible person*.

The call to develop all of man and all men   Man is really a responsible being only when he gives the proper answer to his Creator and Redeemer — the answer that must decide the orientation of his destiny. For every life has its calling, and, in God's plan, every man is called.[12] Called to what? To respond to God's purpose for him and for his brothers by following the plan that outlines his development and that of his brothers. And in God's plan this development is global — it concerns *all of man and all men,* every man in his completeness and all of humanity.[13] What in fact constitutes the launching pad for man in his human condition is therefore the answer he gives to the God who calls him to be. By that answer he becomes a responsible human being.

1. *Responsible Man*

In order to be responsible, man must *listen to God*. For man is called above all to listen to the Word of God,[14] and then to give an answer. But the call and the answer are not located only on the plane of intellectual comprehension. In his Word, God reveals himself as active. His Word is an act of creation and an act of redemption. His Word is effective. It awakens in man a response of total involvement, total consecration of his entire being and all of his history, an effective involvement. It is the whole of man that is addressed. And to such a call man can only answer with his entire being, by a mobilization of all his individual and social characteristics.

Total man   Man is called to life, to action, to the development of his entire being — wholly and without reservation — body, soul and spirit. The Bible is innocent of the pagan dualism that sets soul and spirit over against body and matter, and of that dualism which sets the individual over against society. Man is one. His existence is set in nature and society. The lowest and the highest elements of his being together form the entirety of his person. Body and soul are co-equal; individuals and community are co-equal. A dualistic conception of man and his structure is a false division and an alienation of his true make-up. The Bible sends both materialists and spiritualists packing.[15] Just as foreign to biblical thinking is a purely individualistic conception, isolating the individual from the community, or a collectivistic approach that would accord to the life of the community a privileged position over the individual.

Sacred and secular   It would be an equally great imposture to take the whole man of which the Bible speaks and dissect him into compartments for the sacred and divine, on the one hand, and for the secular and human, on the other. In the Bible, only God is truly sacred, thrice holy (Father, Son and Holy Spirit), whereas all of creation is secular, that is, the product of divine effort, endowed with its existence. But since this existence is viable only if it remains in contact with divinity, man's life — entirely secular — takes on meaning only by contact with divinity. Only God is sacred, while his creation belongs entirely to the secular sphere. Moreover, his intervention by Christ into the world is a secular act to the extent that it excludes any sacralizing act other than itself. For there is not in the world the slightest fragment of sacredness, not the smallest basis for an autonomous, anthropocentric religion. But secularization becomes auto-destructive, an alienating and distorting force, when it makes of creation or mankind their own end and justification, when it relates man's earthly work to other ends than those set for it by Christ. We will return to this point.[16]

Faith and action   Responsible man as described in the Bible responds to his calling by a total commitment of his being. This means that there is no possibility for him to answer on the basis of religious faith alone without an involvement of his acts and his works. Responsible man is the one who answers God's call to him through Christ by a total involvement of his entire history, all his decisions and all his activities — personal, cultural, economic, social and political. Such a commitment is what constitutes religious commitment. Religion rightly defined is not to be found beside or beyond these particular commitments, although in order to direct them it does include specific activities (prayer, attention to the Word of God, etc.). Christ, the model of a humanity entirely responsible in its complete obedience and complete creativity, showed the way to perfect commitment. Because of the exact correspondence of his own free will to that of God,[17] he fulfilled his own destiny perfectly, in a way that conformed to God's plan, all the while freely subject to the divine will. He was freed from all alienating and distorting constraints because he had full control of his liberty, because he was perfectly obedient — of his own free and voluntary will.

As for natural man, secular man, it is by answering Christ's call, by entering freely into Christ's free obedience, by participating freely in the action freely undertaken by Christ, that he fulfils his humanity.[18] Now this action by which man responds to his calling is the expression of his faith and the realization of his obedience. It is what allows for his development and that of his fellows.

2. *Man in Society*

The program God assigns for man's existence is thus a program of development, but of development as understood in the divine plan. That plan requires a scale of values and an order of priorities that correspond to no present plan of development. First of all it has a concern for last things, those things on which all the rest depend. Only a continual search for communion with Christ can ensure the formation of a fully responsible humanity. The result is that the development of one man is inconceivable without the development of all the others. Man is called to participate in a development of his own personality on a par with the personality of everyone else. We must make ourselves, both as individuals and as members of the human race.[19] The goal is the true development of man. Economic and social development is only a part, a necessary part, of man's development. What we are aiming for is the enrichment of the human spirit at all levels, in ourselves and in others.[20]

As for economic development, it necessitates social development in a climate of solidarity. We men are made to be dynamic, progressive, imaginative, adventurous, creative. Our task in the twentieth century, the task of all mankind, is to develop and *share* the riches of the world in such a way that all men may benefit and attain their full human stature.[21]

Finally, this development must be a community development. It implies an interdisciplinary policy in order to ensure global development of all human communities. We cannot claim to know all that is in man or all that is fully human. We know that we must listen to experts in every area of knowledge and collaborate with them. But we do require the development of man, and, as a part of this development, social and economic development, because we believe that man's future is open and that the future of many could be and should be more open than it is now. We believe that all men have the right to self-development, to membership in the community of man. And we dare to think that when we play our part in this work, what we do is a part of the *ongoing creation* of our world by God, is a part of his plan for men.[22]

Development   Man's calling is therefore a call to growth, to growth in the human community. It is important to emphasize once more that the full development of man is not a simple question of economic growth,[23] and that man's true stature may develop only in communion with Christ.[24] But we must also stress that, in God's plan for all creation, this development includes economic growth.

At birth every man receives from God an endowment of aptitudes and qualities to cultivate, and among them is the capacity for work and economic production. The expansion of these aptitudes depends both on the education he receives and on the possibilities provided by environment and personal effort. Gifted with intelligence and freedom, everyone is responsible for his growth. Helped, but also occasionally hindered, by those who educate him and associate with him, each man is the principal artisan of his success or his failure — whatever the influences he undergoes.[25]

But, let us repeat, the growth of each individual is linked to the growth of his fellows, to the mutual community of those many gifts which God has given to his children for the enrichment of human life.[26] For it is God's will to endow everyone with an abundant life.[27] And Christ is a constant witness that human growth according to God's plan is growth for others, prosperity in service for others. With this understanding, any one person can be asked to voluntarily renounce his own economic growth for the overall growth, spiritual and material, of others.

In order to assure the outworking of this plan for equitable human growth, God gave to man the tremendous task of ruling the earth and subduing it.

The dignity of work and of technology   To foster their own development, men are called by God to rule over nature, of which they are themselves a part. Their task, then, consists of mastering both that nature which surrounds them and their own nature. Whereas many primitive religions consider man to be subservient to nature, the God of the Bible summons human beings to take possession of nature and to subdue it so as to satisfy their own legitimate needs. God created man that he might be master of the earth.[28] The incarnation of his Son — the Word made flesh to dwell among us — highlights the supremely important role assigned to man in the divine economy.[29] The order given to man by God, recorded for us on the first page of the Bible ("Fill the earth and subdue it"[30]), shows that all of creation was meant for man. He was charged with putting his mind to work in order to make proper use of it, and, by his work, to bring it, as it were, to its completion in his service.[31] We must note immediately that if such is man's calling from God, it is for him a *right*: he must be assured a portion of productive property. For if the earth was created to furnish each man with means of subsistence and with the necessary means for his progress, today provided for by multi-faceted technology, every man has the right to glean what he needs from the earth.[32] Vatican II made the same point: "God intended the earth and all it contains to be enjoyed by all men and all peoples; thus the wealth of creation must flow equitably to all men, according to the rules of justice and charity."[33]

It must immediately be added that this calling puts limits on man's power over nature, although they may be difficult to establish in practical terms. Though he is instructed to exploit nature, man is also charged with protecting it. She is his sister, loved and living, and not a plaything. She must be respected as an estate that he manages but does not own. He has no right to mistreat her, to abuse her, to annihilate her. These considerations throw light — without providing complete solutions — on the problems so pressing today of the extent of man's right over nature and over his own nature. Creation is subordinate to man, but both are subordinate to God. Thus subordinate, man's liberty is not unconditional: it is authentic, worthy and real only to the extent that it is subordinate to God and in accord with his intentions.

And thus the dignity of work, along with the necessity of technology to carry it through, finds its legitimate basis. And on that basis is also founded the spiritual guarantee of man's right to participate in the common work of mastering and subduing creation by technology. All other rights, whatever they might be, including the rights to property and free enterprise, are subordinate to the initial right, and it is a weighty and urgent social duty to bring them back to their intended purpose when the need arises.[34]

Technological man, vicar of God   In order to assure this general participation of every individual and mankind as a whole in God's creative work, by means of the technological tools man is supposed to create in view of carrying out his mission, it is of primary importance that all of man's cultural, economic and technological efforts be subordinate to the creative power of God himself. This is a particular aspect of man's general calling. We must remember that the great creative development of God in Christ — from the beginning in the Garden of Eden until the creation of the last city,[35] itself a work of civilization and technology and built with nature as its base — presupposes the voluntary and continuous participation of man with the living God and his perpetual submission to God's creative power.[36] God, in Christ, is the Lord of all creation, of nature and of history, the Creator continually creating, and he has chosen man to represent him, to exercise lordship for him over nature entrusted to him. When the Bible tells us that God created man in his image, the whole passage indicates clearly that this implies man's domination of nature,[37] but it is a vicarious domination, itself subject to God's plan.

Far from being condemned to a passive attitude, as is the case in all natural religions, intellectual man with his capacities for creation and invention, his tools and techniques, is promoted to the position of God's vicar, himself a creator under God. He is fully free as a vicar — fully free to carry out his divine charge. His technology is beneficial and his development harmonious just as long as he exercises this deputyship with a full consciousness of his charge, with full awareness of his responsibility as a subordinate.[38] This is what the Churches meant to say when they affirmed that man's full development, including his participation in technological and economic progress, is part of God's *continuing creation* of our world,[39] and that love consists in providing the means, more intelligently than in the past and with more attention to the complex technology involved, for individuals and groups to participate in this development. For God is at work in the development taking place today.[40] Man may, therefore, cooperate with the Creator in completing creation[41] by the work God has commanded him to carry out.[42] And as long as he remains freely and fully submitted to God's liberating will, he will avoid making his work, his technology, his science into self-justifying ends in themselves. Enlightened by the teaching of Christ, he cannot be entranced by the seductive power of progress, technology or science, nor by the seductive power of economic growth.[43]

While contemplating the creating and inventing God, and while submitted to him, the technological spirit, the inventive spirit, the creative, innovative spirit, the spirit of scientific research are all part of man's calling and obedient service.[44] And the principle of modern industrialization has its place in the development of creation as willed by God; it is a fully justified product of this development.[45]

As one may see, this creative, innovative action of a loving God who fosters the complete development of individuals and communities has included within itself scientific and technological research from the stone age down to the present conquest of space.[46] But neither this dynamic quality of the entire creation nor that power which animates human history corresponds to some of the staid theological images that are too widespread among Christians; nor do the evolutionary or mechanistic schemas of modern philosophies that ascribe to man's action as well as to the evolution of nature and of mankind a self-authenticating value, do justice to the facts. There is progress in man's works and in creation that must be ascribed to a plan of the living God. And God constantly summons man to participate in and assume responsibility for this progression.[47]

But this progress is by no means automatic: man is capable of setting up forces counter to progress by using his strength and technical abilities for purposes other than those assigned by God.[48] There is no progress beneficial to man unless his progress is in line with the *dynamic orders* constantly communicated to men by God with the intention of fostering their overall growth until the end of time, until the new creation reaches its fulness. He therefore sets down ethical priorities for men and societies, and these priorities have precedence over the insistent priorities of a technological, economic, commercial, financial or political nature.

Management and distribution   It is not enough to say that man is called by God to subject creation to the divine plan by himself giving in to God's will. As a responsible being, man's duty is to master all of creation. Man's technological vicariate includes not only the permission and duty to explore nature, to unveil its mysteries and to use his knowledge to subject them, in a responsible fashion, to his needs. It also demands that all of this cultural, scientific, technological and economic activity be subject to the divine goal for such activity, that it be perfectly coordinated and always under control. In other words, man is man only to the extent that he remains the master of his own acts and capable of judging their worth, to the extent that, as the author of his own progress, he programs it according to the master-plan assigned by God. For nature — and this is very important — is not a law to itself: it must be *domesticated*. And man has been chosen by God and granted his technological resources for that very purpose. This means that the guiding principle of man's life and activity is not simply liberty for liberty's sake, nor a self-authenticating, voluntary plan and project, but both *liberty and the plan* must be subject to the essential finality of humanity.[49] In other words, good and proper development is not to be equated with selfish culture and wealth cherished for themselves alone. Development means putting all of man's economic action to the service of humanity, distributing daily bread to everyone.[50] Under such conditions, human culture and development, like the fruits of Canaan that symbolized the promised land, that is, God's grace, can in turn become visible demonstrations of God's love toward humanity.[51]

The divine vicariate that man is called to occupy in order to fulfil his own history includes, therefore, beyond the mandate of continuing creation through the arts, sciences and technological advances, that of *management*. Man is neither proprietor nor absolute master of nature and his own works. His calling requires him properly to manage and develop his patrimony according to the goals God set up for the exploitation of his realm: love, brotherhood, solidarity. Thus man's calling requires him to give thought to proper management and just distribution. Care for development and for its practical consequences was assigned to us by our Creator — so the churches declared at Beirut. And he speaks to us through the requests of our brothers for bread, for work, for medical care, for instruction, for human dignity and justice.[52]

We must emphasize immediately that man's responsibility is not limited to the management of his own personal property. Rather, it implies that there is, in the context of human solidarity for development, a collective responsibility of a political nature. We will touch on this later. We are responsible, not only for our own personal status, but also for the political and economic institutions through which the proper management and just distribution of earth's riches are carried out. And today our responsibility has taken on new dimensions. We live in a new world of exciting prospects. For the first time in history, men can consider the unity of humanity to be a reality. The new possibilities of technology transform dreams into realities. The adventure of cooperation with all men for the development of the earth for all men is open for all of us.[53] It is thus by safeguarding, developing and apportioning the resources of creation that we carry out our mandate for management.[54]

Mastering wealth   To sum up, man's increasing store of knowledge, of every kind of artistic and material wealth drawn judiciously from nature's storehouse, is not only a proper thing, but in conformity with God's plan for men and with the calling he has addressed to humanity. But this enrichment is not an end in itself, and is justifiable only in practical terms: if all of man's wealth, both cultural and economic, is controlled and used in the service of all men.[55] All that is necessary is that the growth of wealth leave here and there a few enclaves of poverty, be it individual, social or national, or that it not respect those ethical priorities which are in line with man's calling to global solidarity, for it to be denounced, however legitimate its appearance, as being contrary to God's plan and his love for men.[56] This means, once again, that private property is no man's absolute and unconditional right, and that the use of any possession whatever is legitimate only if he uses it in accordance with God's plan. No one is authorized to keep for his own use what goes beyond his needs while others are lacking basic necessities.[57] The very notion of necessity is in direct relationship to man's call to global solidarity and to the needs of every man. What John says, in line with Christ's teaching, about the communication that must exist between the rich and the poor, and thus about proper management and distribution, is equally applicable for individuals, social groups and nations. God's will does not concern only the behavior of individuals but also that of different societies and the groups that make them up.

The task, therefore, of gaining global control on the technological development of humanity and completely subduing it to human goals voluntarily accepted, is a project that is yet to be accomplished. None of the models of technical society that are presently in operation has provided sufficient mastery of distribution. Nowhere are the essential choices of a people assumed according to a hierarchy of needs explicitly formulated and democratically accepted. The centers of socio-economic decision-making are beyond determination by the people, both in the West and in the East.

Controlled demography   Within the perspective of man mastering nature, it is obvious that man's first task is to master his own nature — throughout all the areas of life. That is particularly true of his mastery of procreation. It is certainly true that God alone gives life and that he continues his work of creation in and through Christ. But it is equally true that he makes use of man's creative and responsibly assumed procreative act, and that man received this gift from God as part of his human liberty. Man's calling to responsibility and to the mastery of his own works includes first of all the inalienable right for every human being to marry and to procreate, a right basic to man's human dignity.[58] It belongs to the parents to decide, in the full knowledge of their circumstances, the number of their children, and to take their responsibilities before God, before themselves and before the children they have already brought into the world.[59] But referring to individual and familial criteria is not enough. The parents' decision is part of a social and historical situation that they must not ignore and which is also a determining factor in deciding their responsibilities. They must also make their decisions with respect to the community to which they belong, and that community has a responsibility toward them.[60] And is it possible to speak of responsible parenthood where subhuman living conditions, such as excessive misery or mental, social or political oppression, with all the vice they spawn, make the exercise of responsibility virtually impossible? Clearly it is impossible to exact or obtain the development of human responsibility in the area of parenthood as long as men are not in favorable circumstances on the other planes of life (social, economic and political).

3. *Responsible Society — Regional and Worldwide*

Everything said about man's creative activity in culture, science, technology and finance requires a collective responsibility; not only a responsibility of each one toward others, but a responsibility shared with others. For all men have the right and the duty to participate in those activities for development which are in accordance with God's plan to form a community with other men.[61] All men share the same humanity, that is, the same calling to fulfilment.[62] For the biblical authors, humanity is a whole, with a common nature and a common destiny. All groups, all tribes, all nations, all races are involved in a single historical development.[63] God's goal is the unification of humanity in wealth as well as in diversity.[64] And never as today have external technological forces exerted such an influence in bringing about the exterior aspects of this unity. Never have the different parts of the world been so bound by such a bond of interdependence, thanks to science and technology. Such a situation invites us to action oriented to the brotherhood of all men.[65] We will see below the practical consequences, political, social, economic and ecclesiastical, of this vigorous proclamation of Scripture in favor of a common destiny for all peoples and all nations, rich in all their diversity.[66]

Two: alienated humanity and its restoration

We have now studied God's plan for man, for society and for all creation, and have reviewed the biblical concept of this great design. Since the beginning, and until the end of time, Christ is at work sustaining all of creation in its advance toward its final goal: transfiguration and fulfilment at the end of time.

This royal progression, however, does not correspond to the various schemas of evolutionary doctrine. It is a permanent drama, one that is played out between God and his creatures. For God gave man liberty — a liberty that enables him, while in permanent communion with his God, to spontaneously accomplish His will. But he also gave him the ability to refuse that liberty and to fall into the slavery of a pseudo-autonomy falsely called liberty.

A. MAN'S FAILURE

This drama, whose breadth and consequences are of cosmic dimensions, may be seen in the burning marks it leaves in the history of each and every man. Its seriousness and depth are revealed in the life, death and resurrection of Christ: these attest to the fundamental corruption of God's work by adverse powers, but also to its permanent recuperation, its transformation, its redemption, and finally its glorification — the fruits of victorious love. The marks of this drama are visible in the history of man, and also in creation. For besides the laws of growth and development, harmony and order, one sees in nature the laws of murder, suffering and violence. *Nature is therefore ambiguous.* It is the mother of mankind, but also its enemy. It produces thorns and thistles, hurricanes, floods, droughts, earthquakes, famines and all the monstrous crimes that accompany them. And man finds within himself, within his own nature, not only laws of life, but also laws of destruction that deform him and turn him from his calling and toward death. All of creation is ambiguous, and the laws that govern nature and the life of humanity are also, therefore, laws of distortion, destruction and death. The natural and the social sciences reveal to us these ambiguous and contradictory laws. There is no such thing as a "natural order," stable and harmonious, either for the outside world, for man, or for human society. Such is the reality that history permits us to glimpse and which the Bible shows us clearly.[1]

1. *Alienated Man*

As an integral part of the cosmic drama, man may be led to refuse the calling addressed to him by God and thus to lose his freedom, the essential element of his humanity. He can go about it in several ways.

The alienation of man without God   First of all, as we just mentioned, man may refuse to listen and hear the call God directs toward him. This refusal leads to all the accumulated forms of alienation. If man is unaware that his goal is not within himself, nor in nature, nor in history, nor in humanity, nor in anything created, he begins to think that he is himself his goal. Or he supplies his destiny with all kinds of religious or ideological goals that are foreign to his true destiny. Economic wealth, unlimited confidence in science and technology, self-sufficient economic growth, nationalism, and ideologies liberal, capitalist, socialist and communist — to the extent that they are considered self-authenticating goals — are today the most common forms of collective alienation.

The alienation of religious man   But there are also partial alienations that slip into the very heart of man's response to the call of the living God. The most frequent form in the history of Christianity is that of spiritual dualism. We have already mentioned how important it is for man to know that he is fully involved in the existence God has outlined for him — body, soul and spirit. A man who has been split apart, spirit to one side and matter to the other, whose religious faith does not include his physical, corporal, sexual, professional, economic and political existence, is an alienated man whose life both temporal and eternal is doomed to failure by that very alienation. The separation of the sacred from the profane within human life and within society, and the opposition set up between the temporal and the eternal belong to the same type of alienation. A slightly different alienation, very frequent within contemporary Christianity, stems from a too radical separation between faith and action, faith and works, faith and political or economic decisions. The Gospel undoubtedly emphasizes the priority of decision by faith in all human behavior. But this faith is authentic only to the extent that it involves man in his entirety, as a historical being, both flesh-and-blood and spiritual, individual and social, conjugal, familial, political, economic.

Useful secularization   Nonetheless, the form of human alienation that is today most current is secularization. If the term is understood as denoting the historical process of declericalization, that is, for Western history, the progressive freeing of man from all forms of ecclesiastical tutelage and religious imperialism within cultural, political, social and economic life, it is obvious that this form of secularization is beneficial. And this benefit, even if it has often developed historically as total opposition to Christianity in a struggle against certain of its abuses and distortions, is a direct outcome of Christianity properly understood, of Christ's own message, however paradoxical that might appear. If we understand secularization as this action of authentic Christian faith against all forms of religious subterfuge that impeded, and still impede, the free development of humanity, the free access of men and women to artistic, scientific and technical activity, and to social and political responsibility, it is obvious that this phenomenon is progress. Man's response to God's call to him through Christ, a call that invites him to participate in the general work of promoting humanity, includes, as we have already stated, removing the sacred from the zone of creation, the desacralization of God's entire creation.

A secularization that alienates   But an alienating secularization is one that tries to remove this properly secular creation from the destiny God assigned it when he subordinated it to Christ's existence and cosmic work. The deadly consequences of this secularization are innumerable because, by keeping man from understanding and fully carrying out his calling, they lead to the loss of his humanity and to the destruction of all humanity. It is a pseudo-secularization that is in fact a double *secularization,* an unconscious deification (a secular sacralization of secularization!). In it, man or creation is considered its own goal. Man is then no longer able to fulfil his calling as a vicar, entrusted with developing and managing all of creation in God's name. He attributes to his work a mystical value and it ends up crushing and devouring him.[2] The technology that he builds as an instrument of his domination turns against him and becomes the means of enslaving him and distorting him.[3] (We will touch on this point again.)

The economic progress and development that were supposed to ensure his prosperity and that of all men have, without any quantitative or qualitative norms, no standard but profit (individual, collective, national) and become a source of exploitation and misery.[4] And the legitimate enrichment that man was supposed to acquire by responding to his divine calling brings out coveteousness within him and breaks the harmony and solidarity that should have produced a general enrichment to the exclusion of poverty.[5] In sum, all the powers with which God entrusted him, to ensure his rule over nature and society, his scientific, political and economic powers, are degraded. He uses them to exploit others, thereby destroying the harmony of social life.[6] And alienated man, as a result of a calling that was missed or distorted by a false conception of religion, has developed a degraded and corrupt society.

2. *A Dissolute Society*

Man's inability to give a responsible answer to the call addressed to him by God is a result of a break in communication with the living God. This leads to a drying up of the source of love — the only cement capable of building human societies and holding them together. Loss of love results in the slow death of society in general.

The anti-humanism of a closed humanity   The world ends up dying from lack of charity. The evil consists less in the sterilization of resources, or in their being taken over by a minority, than in the lack of brotherhood between individuals and between peoples.[7] Of course, man can organize the world without God, but without God he can in fact organize it only against man.[8] For a closed humanity, shut off from God, an exclusive humanity, is an inhuman humanity.[9] The same is true of a religious humanism shut off from humanity.[10]

From this break in communication between man and life-giving love come all the forms of degradation that corrupt man's life within society. And they are legion. Modern ecumenical studies have not been content with denouncing sins and evils in a general, anonymous way, nor with reducing them to their individual or purely religious proportions, as too many theologians and preachers do. They have described very explicitly the instances and forms of this degradation.

The perversion of technology   One form is technology itself. Born of the marvelous power given to man to enable him to conquer and master nature, it can also become a tool of destruction in his hands. Subject to no outside authority, since man himself has forgotten his place in God's plan, technology has become ambiguous, ambivalent, as often destructive as it is constructive. Instead of making judicious use of it in subjecting nature, man's practice has rather been toward dissolution and madness. He devours natural resources until they are exhausted. He wipes out the open spaces that were meant to provide him with a harmonious habitat. His industries pollute air and water. He is incapable of intelligently organizing the land he occupies. He insanely contaminates all of nature with radioactivity — over which he has already lost control. With his own nature uncontrolled, and incapable of controlling his environment, he hands the earth and its riches over to the reckless conquest of private interests, party interests or national interests — themselves confused and pushed into hasty action by the incoherent pressure of unbridled population growth. Incapable of exercising technological control over the marvelous riches entrusted to him by God, incapable of the coherent management that would have assured him continued control, he abandons them to a kind of brigandage where the strongest, the richest, the toughest triumph at the expense of the weak and the poor. Whereas control over nature was supposed to satisfy harmoniously both the legitimate needs of God's children and respect for nature itself; whereas technology was supposed to enable man to eliminate hunger and poverty from the earth, we see man putting this technology to selfish, personal, social, political or national ends, to satisfy his own anxiety, pride or blind spirit of rivalry, a morbid and destructive form of healthy competition.

Technology in warfare   War and preparation for war are by far the greatest promoters of technology. There is much more available money, concerted action, intelligent cooperation, exemplary unselfishness and passionate zeal in the conquest of space and in military preparations than in the struggle against misery, illiteracy and underdevelopment. And atomic fission, with all its unpredictable promise, is put to a much greater use in the preparation of means of destruction than for bettering humanity.

Manipulated man   Moreover, man himself as the object of this uncontrolled technology is threatened by his own marvelous discoveries. He can easily be manipulated and transformed in a thousand ways, even to the depths of his very soul. His conscience can be molded, not only by his pharmaceutical products but also by his interference in the genetic code. It is true that science, technology and industry have given man more and more liberty from his servitude to nature and from his most pressing needs, but man is nonetheless mechanized and subject to the laws of his own tools — he is jostled and out of his element. He becomes a function and a product of his own work. Instead of being subject to nature, he has become a slave of his uncontrolled tools, which were meant to give him domination over nature. Partially freed, in industrial societies, from the effort and fatigue of production, he becomes the fatigued and sickly prey of the consumer society. And already one can perceive threatening signs of massive destruction of the human race by nuclear warfare or by degeneration.

   In truth, the ambiguous nature of technology and its harmful results are only the results of man's own objective situation when he does not fully accept his divine calling. The damage wrought by technology is only the product of man's basic alienation. He communicates to his tools the characteristics of his own degradation.[11]

The corruption of power   If this is true of technology, it is no different with the growing powers this technology has given to men — economic power, social power, political power. Because man has refused both the obedience and responsibility that go along with his sonship, according to the Churches at Uppsala, his God-given dominion has degenerated into exploitation and all his relations have degenerated into alienation.[12] For this reason we live in a world where man, instead of using his powers in service of others, endeavors on the contrary to exploit his neighbor.[13]

The illusion of a natural or historical order   Such is especially the case where men, unconcerned with learning God's will for the world, trust in *the laws of nature or history* to direct their political, economic and social relations. However, we have already seen the ambiguous nature of these laws (proved by scientific research) : although in certain of their aspects they do create development, prosperity and harmony, in others they generate violence, murder and pillage.[14] Intended to weave the harmonious yet complex web of social ties necessary to build up societies, they can also, by giving free rein to the oppressive aggressiveness of the rich and the strong, destroy these social ties and subject all of society to the law of selfish individualism or of selfish collectivism. The greed of individuals, families and nations can captivate the poor like the rich and generate in both a strangling materialism.[15]

The perversion of uncontrolled freedom   The same is true when liberty is sought after for its intrinsic value and is not accepted as subject to God's will. It can then engender economic dictatorship by the richest individuals, the strongest political parties and the most powerful nations.

It is not enough to augment common wealth in order to spread it equitably. It is not enough to foster technology to make the earth more humane to live upon.[16]

The illusion of liberalism   On the other hand, trusting in a supposed natural order to organize and harmonize human life leads to a liberal capitalism supported by an ideology consisting of this very pretension. It leads to suffering, to injustice, and at last to those fratricidal struggles which have become a part of contemporary history.[17] Neither profit, as the essential motivating power of economic progress, nor rivalry as the supreme law of economics, nor private ownership of the means of production as an absolute right, with no concomitant social limits or obligations, can by themselves engender a harmonious social and economic life. Given over to such laws, economic developments can lead only to an international imperialism of money,[18] to oppressive structures resulting from the abuse of possessions or power, to the exploitation of the worker, to injustice in commercial transactions,[19] and finally to the rule of hunger, undernourishment, underdevelopment and discouragement.[20]

The illusion of collectivism   But it would be just as false to imagine that other types of social, political and economic life, founded on other ideologies than that of a supposed natural order and just as ignorant of the different forms taken by God's will for man and for society, are able to provide for men a well-ordered human condition. Passing from a liberal ideology that pushes the principle of liberty beyond its limits, to a collectivistic ideology that denies the principle of liberty, will change only the environment of injustice, exploitation and abuse of power — they will not themselves be changed.[21]

Toward economic democracy   Experience has shown that while, in a free economy, economic decisions and the basic choices that direct the life of a people are made by hidden minorities that completely escape control by the nation (the decisions of the marketplace are made only by solvent consumers who have been radically propagandized by the subtle forces of advertising), these decisions and choices are no more democratic in a country with a centralized economy. There also, they are imposed by a minority whose acts are not subject to popular approval. A form of democratic economy that would submit the basic choices of global development to the conscious will of the people has yet to be invented. Such a democracy would be especially valuable in enabling Christians to transform into concrete goals what they think corresponds to God's economic plan in a given time and place and to submit these goals to popular approval. Establishing a democratic economic system goes hand in hand with the development of an industrial democracy that would permit all the partners in work to participate in the major decisions concerning them. Legislative powers must of course be well separated from executive powers.

Degradation of institutions   In reality, the inability of man to respond fully to his calling leads to a profound perversion not only of man himself but of all his *institutions.* Just as the degradation of technology is a reflection of alienated man, so does this alienation touch all the institutions created for the proper functioning of social life. The subjective evil that is in man creates objective evil in his institutions. We live in a world where man exploits man, we know the reality of sin and the depth of its hold on human beings. Political and economic structures groan under the weight of grave injustice.[22] And one of the forms taken by this corruption of political and social institutions, the Churches point out, is their resistance to change. The routine of life and a spirit of conservatism, ruling the emotions of men afraid of the future, keep them from carrying out the necessary reforms.[23]

Inequality and injustice   The accumulated results of this dissipation of individuals and institutions become manifest in the terrible injustice and inequality that exist today, both between continents and within a given nation. Such conditions are absolutely unconscionable.[24] They appear in the endless greed of the rich, individuals and nations, and even in flourishing civilizations that selfishly turn inward. The Gospel teaches that such greed and selfishness call down both the judgments of God and the wrath of the poor, with unpredictably terrible consequences.[25]

Revolutionary violence or reactionary violence?   Indeed, such is one of the most certain causes of the unleashing of violence in today's world and of the resultant revolutions. This violence and these revolutions in turn spawn new injustices, introduce new inequalities and bring new disasters. They are both the cause and the effect of the basic corruption of men and of institutions.[26]

In analyzing these facts, the Churches have shown more discernment than on occasion in the past. They are no longer

content with a unilateral condemnation of revolutionary violence. Rather they have seen that often, as a result of the
corruption in men and institutions in certain particularly
oppressive regimes, there exist hidden forms of violence within
the very fabric of these regimes and in the legal measures they
enact to maintain the status quo and respect for "law and
order" (even if this order goes by a revolutionary title). This
type of restraint, imposed on certain minorities, forcing their
acquiescence to the majority or vice versa, in time brings about
violent efforts at change.[27]

Conservative or reactionary violence, alongside revolutionary violence, is among the most common plagues in all areas
of today's world. Few peoples can boast of not having them
and few Christians can claim not to be accomplices in one or
the other of them. In such circumstances it is astonishing that
the Churches have not ascribed more importance to the development of nonviolent action.

Among the factors leading to corruption and violence
most widespread today must be mentioned racism.

Racism   Racism is often prevalent in young nations, where
it is frequently hidden under clan or political rivalries, to the
great injury of justice and at the risk of civil war.[28] But young
nations have no monopoly on this plague. Racism was rampant during the colonial era, setting colonists and natives at
odds, provoking much bitterness as the consequence of real injustices. And it is prevalent today, here, there and everywhere,
more or less latent according to the region.

White racism   What racism appears most often today in unconscious forms during attempts at collaboration between rich
and underdeveloped nations. But it becomes a festering source
of division and implacable hate when it settles within a state
that, in defiance of the inviolable rights of the human being,
unjustly submits individuals and families to a regime of discrimination because of their race or color.[29] White racism is
often an aggressive force that impedes and warps development.
The feeling of white superiority — a manifestation of spiritual
illness and underdevelopment — degrades humanity and keeps
one from establishing intelligent relations with persons of
another color. When this racism takes on institutional forms,

as is the case in certain regions, when it becomes a part of the political, pedagogical and economic system, it animalizes those who suffer the discrimination. It prevents them from expanding as human beings, as citizens and as participants in the economic life of the nation.[30]

Today's racism, then, constitutes a source of violence capable of unleashing the greatest disorders. It removes all meaning from human rights and is an imminent menace to world peace.

Racism is a flagrant travesty of the work Christ has undertaken in the world for the development of individuals and of mankind in general. It is a denial of the original unity of mankind predicated in the universal work of redemption Christ came to carry out in order to restore to all men without distinction the effaced image of God.

Racism manifests its corrupting nature by the very arguments it uses to justify itself: fallacious generalizations and untruths that lead to the denigration of persons, to segregation and to all forms of separatism.

Counter-racism   Its noxious nature becomes even more obvious in the fact that it produces a counter-racism that is only a defensive measure of human survival. And it also perpetuates from generation to generation the illusions and lies of racism.[31] (It is important not to mistake counter-racism, which is the racist reply of oppressed races, for the healthy and necessary struggle against racism.)

Irresponsible procreation   Responsible procreation is one mark of human intelligence in those who have understood the harmonious destiny to which God calls men and societies, but irresponsible procreation and unplanned parenthood, distrust of family planning subordinate to God's will, show just how irresponsible man can be when he does not take his calling seriously, or when he is the desperate prey of overpowering misery. This irresponsibility, a sign and usually the effect of his degradation, entails the suffering and disruption of the family. It thus contributes to the duration of social misery. Such irresponsibility can, moreover, lead both to unrestricted population growth and to a Malthusian population control that maintains an insufficient density of active human forces.

Nationalism   Finally, one of the most typical social diseases that characterize man's inhumanity and his refusal of the divine call is nationalism. Though it is a fact that nationalism has often been a constructive force for unification, especially in the building phase of a young nation where it can make a community out of tribal, ethnic or territorial groups, and though nationalism can also help in stimulating creative cultural forces as well as a proper desire for independence from outside tyranny, be it political, economic or cultural, it is often one of the most active causes of division and destruction at work in the world, both within nations and between them. It is often an *idolatry of the nation,* a characteristic perversion of man's calling to live within a pluralistic and universal humanity, a calling made manifest in Christ's work.[32] In truth, nationalism isolates peoples to their own detriment and destroys the solidarity of nations.[33]

Often it only masks national selfishness by making moral underdevelopment into a virtue.[34] Is the exaltation of nationalism not generally considered an uncommonly great virtue within a nation while it may be only a dangerous form of collective childishness? These diverse forms of nationalism introduced into international relations bring about a weakening of will among the rich countries, mostly situated in the northern hemisphere, to cooperate with the poor countries, frequently in the southern hemisphere.[35]

The arms race   Moreover, nationalism is one of the most murderous agents in international conflicts. It leads to the arms race, sapping the strength of innumerable countries and itself a bearer of terrible dangers, "an intolerable scandal," denounced and condemned (unfortunately more in theory than in practice) by all churches.[36] The immorality of this headlong race is most visible in the fact that it is a preparation for the massive destruction of humanity; then in the fact that it consumes wealth that is not taken from a nation's surplus, but in most cases from the little put aside for national development. Or, among the richer nations, military budgets take the resources that could be used in aiding the development of weaker nations.[37] The fact that this scandal appears "normal" or inevitable to peoples and governments attests clearly to what extent man is losing his humanity.[38] Moreover, the fact that so many Christians are untouched by, or, even worse, voluntarily involved in this process, which they consider to be inevitable, shows to what extent the Churches have, practically speaking, quit taking seriously the Gospel and God's will for mankind to live that is expressed there. Do our Churches not take affairs of state, no matter how important they may be, as *more* important than the requirements and promises of the Gospel? And do their choices, once this order of priorities is established, not lose all conformity to the mission of the Churches?

3. *The Judgment of God*

The signs of degradation we have just enumerated, these marks of sin, are only partial and superficial witnesses of corruption. They are only external symptoms of the deeper evil — the break in communication between man and the God of love who became manifest in Jesus Christ, and the calling man has missed, thereby entailing the failure of God's plan for humanity and for all of creation. This failure appears in all its immenseness upon the cross of Golgotha. There one may realize the result of the violence and radical perversion hidden in man, the one who refuses God's call and crucifies his Son. There one may glimpse the nature of the judgment God has chosen to mete out on humanity, repudiating this alienation and refusing the failure by condemning them. For what God wants most of all is the eternal and temporal salvation of his created beings. Thus, by refusing their corruption and condemning it he himself undertakes their restoration.

B. THE FIRST SIGNS OF A NEW WORLD

Although man, incapable of responding to the call of God, thereby loses his identity and then his humanity, the living God who created him and calls him to life does not resign himself to it. He sees man's inability to understand his destiny and to realize his earthly mission, and he suffers along with men. And his love is made manifest in this very refusal to accept the failure of man, and in his condemnation of that failure. Christ's death on the cross, where he took the place of the entire guilty human race, is proof of God's permanent will to save, to reconstruct, and to restore a meaning to all of humanity and all of creation.

God re-creates the world   It was thus to build this new world, a brand new world, completely re-created, and to give humanity a new lease on life, to reclaim its identity, to recover its humanity and to fulfil its destiny again, that God intervened in history by the gift of his Son, by the creation of a New Man, the figure and the model of an entire new humanity.

God and man rejoin   And it is also the lost image of its God that the Creator, by Christ, returns to his creation. For, by losing himself, by losing his true nature, man deprives himself of the very possibility of hearing and returning to his God. The saving Christ is the Christ who reveals the Creator God and the Redeemer God.

It is these essential truths which underlie everything to-day's Churches are saying about their mission in the world. Man is wandering lost because he does not know who he is, proclaimed the Churches at Uppsala. But God is making everything new. And the Bible shows us that in Christ "the New Man" appears and demands our decision.[39]

The future has already begun   Yes, in Christ, God entered our world, its structures and its institutions, and he has gained the victory over all "principalities and powers." His kingdom is coming and, with it, his judgment and his mercy.[40]

By him, God proclaims the liberating word. Hear him say: I go before you. Christ takes away your past sins. The Spirit gives you the freedom to live for others. Anticipate my Kingdom in joyful worship and daring acts. The Lord says, "I make all things new."[41] And this promise is not for an imaginary beyond; it is for a new world that begins here and now.[42]

1. *The Fundamental Structure of All Creation: Polemics and Dialog*

The cross of Christ shows us that the New Man realizes his destiny by a constant battle against what is condemned to die within the old man. Good Friday and Easter show that the new world is to be built on the ruins of the old.

A distorted nature   This means that there is no longer in man a nature that God can recognize as his true nature. What is true and genuine within him, what God accepts, what makes up his true humanity, is what is newly created, what has already been transformed in this world while awaiting its final transfiguration at the end of time.

A radically new creation   And Christ's resurrection also shows that this transfiguration brings something radically new to the old world, to the old man, to the old nature. There is not only a restoration of the old, but a new outreach and fulfilment in an environment of both discontinuity and continuity, of discontinuity fostering continuity.[43] This means that the transformation of the world, which will be radical in the last days, has already begun and is going forward in human history by a prophetic anticipation of the end.

A continual struggle between life and death   This permanent process of mutation, this continual renewal, this fundamental transformation is, therefore, the product of an unceasing struggle. The life, death and resurrection of Christ show that God is engaged in a daily battle against the evil that is defacing his creation, against principalities and powers of all kinds that are constantly at work in the history of this provisional period of earth's history trying to hamper the harmonious development of mankind. Christ's triumph in this struggle shows that he is victorious and that the entire world's hope may be founded on his victory. But the battle goes on, with no respite. Men, mankind, and all of creation reach their true identity and nature only by joining the thick of this battle.

The polemical make-up of the world   Man's basic make-up today, as well as that of society and the entire creation, is, therefore, one of polemics.

But this struggle is not just any combat: it is the permanent combat led by God, in Christ, for the whole universe. It is his ongoing work of renewal for his entire creation. This struggle puts God and his work, on the one side, face to face with man's degrading and distorting nature, animated by the multiple powers of degradation, on the other. Man and creation, then, are involved in this combat only to the extent that they join in the battle waged by God for them. It is a singular combat — on God's side a battle of love, with his only arms, both spiritual and temporal, the arms of love. On man's side, the struggle is waged by a degrading aggressiveness that wields the vilest of arms against God and against his temporal work of re-establishing humanity.[44]

The dialectic nature of man   So man is never alone. And true humanism can never again be a closed humanism. Man can never be truly himself except in this divine face-to-face, in this continual dialog with God, in this battle with God against the destructive and anti-human forces at work in the world. The fundamental structure of the world, then, which enables man to survive and to be transformed for the new life, is one based on dialog. Man and creation can recover existence, be reborn to life, victoriously pass through the judgment and condemnation of God, and benefit from his transfiguring grace only by means of this renewed dialog, the meeting with God that Christ, the New Man who stands before God for all of humanity, has set up as a permanent institution for the entire world.[45]

The victims of combat   Two remarks must be made here which are important for the comprehension of our existence and of our historical action on this earth. In this combat, which has already been victoriously accomplished by Christ but which has only begun in the history of humanity, the victorious Christ already stands at the side of the victims, of all the victims of evil here below, of the victims of all the forms of evil. He is beside those victims who give in to evil and thus accomplish it, but also beside the victims of those who accomplish the evil — for every man is now one, now the other of these victims, whether he knows it or not. And he is a victim whether by his own fault, or by that of the unjust structures and institutions of society with which he collaborates more or less directly. Christ suffers with all these victims. In his death he carries the burden of their condemnation. This means that in human history there can no longer be an absolute criminal. The worst sadist, the most hateful tyrant, the cruelest torturer, the most irresponsible military ruler may one day benefit from Christ's pardon.

The end of crusades   This means that within human history there can no longer be a mystical, violent crusade that is justi-fiable. There can no longer be an enemy so identified with absolute evil that one could wish his eradication for fear that he might attain radical omnipotence in evil. Any attempt to lay on any man or group of men, whoever they may be, the responsibility of absolute evil, any denunication of a given race, class, nation or social group as an irreducible enemy, is doomed to failure as an enterprise of diabolical porportions. On the hill of Golgotha Christ has already taken on himself the condemnation of the criminal most dangerous to mind, body, or body politic, and at Easter he announced the possi-bility of pardon and transfiguration.

The end of messianisms   The other side of the coin: in this unrelenting combat against the creeping forces that degrade man, against all forms of nihilism, oppression, alienation, against all tyrannies, against all ideologies, because the victory has been gaintd once and for all by Christ and by him alone, there can never again appear in human history an absolute messiah, a liberator, a prodigy or a superman capable of granting humanity a liberation more definitive or more com-plete than Christ's. No race, no nation, no social class can claim to grant the world a definitive salvation. Thus all forms of historical messianism are, in their claim to absolutism, illusory, fraudulent and tottering, like any other crusade. Now there can be only temporal campaigns of a relative nature, occasionally necessary, but never definitive, only heroes or despots of relative importance, to be glorified or resisted within the relative frame of current history, never to be heeded as having the last word on hùman destiny.

2. *The New Man: True Man, Complete Man*

As a result of the upheavals that have occurred everywhere during these last decades, men everywhere are trying to under-stand who man is, whence he came and where he is going. And, without a convincing answer, the youth are claiming the freedom to experience human life in all areas, hoping to dis-cover all its aspects and all its riches and thus to find their identity. And the most important choices before our contempo-raries, whether spiritual, religious, cultural, social, economic or political, must be made almost entirely on the basis of the more or less conscious answer they give to the question: Who is man?

To this question — while trying humbly to uncover the innumerable new implications and the diverse consequences of their answer — the Christian Churches reply: Jesus Christ, in his life, death and resurrection, is the true Man.

The true image of God   The authentic human being, formed in God's image, is revealed in him. He is man *par excellence,* because he glorified God by perfect obedience. And because of this obedience, in his complete devotion to others, in his total involvement and absolute liberty, in his penetrating truthfulness and in his victorious acceptance of suffering and death, we see what man is destined to be. At his resurrection a new creation was born and the final goal of human history was made clearly manifest: Christ, the New Man, leader of a new humanity, first-fruits of the new creation, sums up in himself the destiny of all things.[46] And he is at work until creation, which is his work, reaches its full stature and realizes its fulness.[47]

The true form of man   His relation as man with God his Father shows us what man is called to be and what makes true humanity: spontaneously doing God's will, doing it freely and totally.[48]

Freedom in obedience   Throughout Christ's life, and including even his death, we may see human freedom and filial obedience to God linked in a remarkable fashion. To be truly a man does not mean being the toy of a tyrannical deity, nor doing automatically what God himself does. It means freely accomplishing one's own work, while voluntarily fitting it into God's plan. And this is the only way man can recover his basic authenticity, his dignity and his liberty. No longer is he the toy of hidden forces who would turn him from God and make him the butt of his own uncontrolled passions, be they individual, political or national. The end of man's deep alienation is found in Christ.

Liberty in poverty   This reformation is most evident in

Christ's voluntary descent to the level of, and in favor of the poor, showing his full liberty with respect to any domination by economic power. It is not a question of his scorning wealth; rather it is one of giving concrete evidence of his sovereign liberty toward the tyrannical power that all forms of wealth can exercise.[49] And the concrete behavior that corresponds to this liberty is his voluntary abasement among the poor and the oppressed, and his desire to personally effect their liberation.

Liberty for the oppressed   The Word of God attests a Christ who sacrificed himself for his brothers. It shows that Christ stands at the side of the poor and oppressed.[50] And the Churches recognize that Christ's abasement for the poorest of men, and his desire to deliver them from their inhuman condition, is evident in the combat the victorious Christ leads against the "principalities and powers" who interfere not only in men's hearts but also in the structures and institutions of temporal society.[51]

Temporal liberty for all   The fundamental remedy Christ applies to man's alienation by his victory is therefore not only of a spiritual nature: it takes in all levels of temporal restoration known throughout history.[52] In Christ man's future has already begun, is already here, is fulfilled in the warp and woof of temporal history wherever men, consciously or not, join in the struggle for real progress and true liberty for humanity.

This new creation, made manifest and inaugurated in Christ, many aspects of which we have yet to examine, is therefore a dynamic and ongoing phenomenon. It offers new strength to all mankind. It presents a new calling.

3. Man's New Calling

God's intervention into the history of this world through Christ offers men a new perspective. It enables them to answer God's call anew, but this time with new strength, communicated to them by the Holy Spirit.

Recovering his humanity   Man can thus recover and realize his full humanity by joining in the life of the One who has already fulfilled it for him. The possibility is given to all men to be re-established in their position as sons. It is thus essential today to present God's mission as the gift of a new creation, a radical renewal of what is old and an invitation addressed to men to grow to the level of their full humanity in the New Man, Jesus Christ.[53] The new humanity is a gift and, like all of God's gifts, must be accepted by a response of faith. The Holy Spirit offers this gift to man's decision on the most varied occasions. It is the Holy Spirit who takes God's word and makes it a living, converting word to men.[54]

As for the new life, offered freely as a gift of divine grace, it enables man to glimpse what he will be in the fulness of his future regeneration and already to pick out the harbingers of the coming Kingdom.

The decision to be a man   Christ, "the New Man," is calling for our decision[55] because God wants us to become a part of his new humanity.[56] But, at the same time, this participation in Christ's life and combat which we are offered as a gift assumes that we will immediately accept our part in a struggle that will touch all aspects of our existence. It instantly transforms our moral and social behavior.[57]

A political decision   This transformation necessarily has political dimensions.

It especially involves us in efforts to plug the widening gap between the rich and the poor and to struggle in a concrete fashion against the arms race.[58] For every denial of human dignity is in fact a denial of Jesus Christ himself and contradicts any artful profession of faith.[59]

A decision to struggle   Man's calling thus proves to be a calling to combat in Christ's army, and it gives his entire existence a polemical nature.[60–61] But this is a combat which, even if it entails death, is victorious because it is one manifestation of the combat victoriously led by Christ against "the principalities and powers."[62]

A decision to dialog   Because it is a combat at Christ's side, man's calling is to engage in permanent dialog, to feel constantly the need of searching out, listening to, and keeping God's Word, of living before him and in communion with him.

Man's vocation is therefore to accomplish a mission. He is a messenger, charged with proclaiming and witnessing throughout his existence, by every aspect of his life, by his behavior, his words and his acts, to what God has undertaken through Christ for the full development of humanity.[63]

4. Global Renewal[64]

We have spoken, as regards man's calling, of God inviting man to become whole, to live out his faith in the fulness of his existence, in the completeness of his being, body and soul. But we also spoke of man's inability to answer this call, of his inability to live out fully his humanity. And we mentioned the disastrous consequences that result for himself, for all of society and, finally, for all of creation.

But we also saw that God's great love for his creation would not allow him to accept failure. In Christ, he intervened in history in order to inaugurate a new humanity. It is thus by Christ that man is henceforth called once again to fulfil his calling as a man. By this New Man, Christ himself, God opens up again to man the way to his humanity and gives him the power of becoming a man.[65]

In Christ, God gives man new hope and the possibility of personal development. For in Christ there is forgiveness and the possibility of beginning anew every day.[66]

The possibility of renewal   Degenerate man receives from Christ the New Man not only the image of what he is destined to be, but also the possibility of attaining it. To do so, he must allow himself to be transformed, renewed, to the very depths of his being, including the totality of his existence, by the Spirit of Christ, God's Holy Spirit. The new humanity is not only a goal; it is also a gift. And, like all of God's gifts, it must be appropriated by a response of faith.[67] It is this gift of the Holy Spirit and man's gesture of faith which work out the renewal of man in the image of the New Man.

The battle for oneself and for others   We must constantly be taken from the limited, perverted life of the "old man." We must "put on the new man," and this change is always embodied in some actual change of attitude and relationship.

For there is no turning to God that does not at the same time bring a man face to face with his fellow-men in a new way. The new life, by breaking the barriers of race, nationalism, religious bigotry and all others that divide humanity, liberates man and enables him to form a new community existence.[68] The Churches have correctly insisted on the global nature of this renewal, which is too often considered only from the point of view of that religious interiority called "spirituality." Since it is a question of man's original calling being renewed, his calling requires an involvement of the entire man, body and soul, spirit and matter. It aims for the complete development of men, and for human solidarity in global development.[69]

A global view of development   As may be seen, this renewal implies a new understanding of man's entire culture, of all his relationships with nature and with society. It brings the fulness of true development for all men, and this is the bridge for each individual and for all men from subhuman conditions to a genuine human situation.[70]

We have been entrusted with a message and a ministry that go beyond material needs, but we must never allow ourselves to attribute a secondary position to these material and social needs as compared with our responsibilities toward spiritual needs.

There is, then, a burning relevance today in describing the mission of God, of which we are a part, as the gift of a new creation that is a radical renewal of what is old and an invitation to mankind to grow into the fulness of humanity in the New Man, Jesus Christ.[71] True human development is the aim. Economic and social development is a necessary part of this. What we search for is the enrichment of the human spirit at all levels, in ourselves and in others.[72]

There is no authentic confession of faith without practical involvement   We must emphasize that all confessions of faith, all religious discourse and all verbal testimony that are not accompanied by significant concrete action in favor of development and peace, against inequality and against the arms race, locally and globally, are negative testimonies with a powerful negative influence. Such, say the Churches, is today's decisive challenge. God forces us to recognize that Chris-

tians who, by their behavior, deny any dignity to their neighbors, thereby deny Jesus Christ himself, in spite of their profession of faith. We desire, then, united with men of all confessions, to combat for man's rights in a just world community.
We are working, for example, to attain disarmament and the
establishment of economic agreements that are equitable for
all parties. We are ready to tax ourselves in furtherance of a
system of world taxation for development.[73]

Fighting misery and struggling against injustice are the
best means of promoting the human and spiritual progress of
all, and thus the common good of humanity. Peace may not
be defined as an absence of war, the result of a precarious
equilibrium of forces. It is rather something built up day after
day, in the pursuit of an order willed by God, with a more
perfect form of justice among men.[74]

5. *The Restoration of Society*

Man's humanity, then, becomes a reality only by his active
involvement in the evolving future of society. Man's all-encom-
passing call requires that he participate voluntarily and consciously in the creative dynamics of history, in the integral renewal of society. The restoration of man in Christ may not
take place without the restoration of all humanity in Christ.[75]

The continual renewal of institutions   This restoration includes a renewal of political, economic and social institutions.
We discover our true humanity by working with others to
change outmoded institutions and to create new wealth. We
salute this world of change in which we see God constantly at
work, destroying the ways of sin, restoring, re-animating, renewing. "Things which were cast down are being raised up,
things which had grown old are being made new, and all things
are moving toward perfection through him from whom they
took their origin, even Jesus Christ"[76] (from a fourth-century
prayer in the Gelasian Sacramentary) .

As may be seen, Christ's coming means not only the birth
of a New Man but also the inauguration of a Kingdom, that
is, a social renewal that penetrates to the very heart of societal
life and gives the possibility of full renewal.

The Christ who has conquered all the powers of human

degradation, alienation, destruction and a distorted humanity, has been transfigured by his resurrection and is already exercising his sovereignty over the entire world in order to direct it toward the new life that provides finality for all of creation.

As in a mirror, the image of the last tomorrow   Of course the world, blinded by the powers of darkness, has not yet recognized this finality. It is hidden from the world, but is not thereby deprived of its effectiveness.

And Christians themselves, who make up the Church, are victims of this blindness, are not yet benefitting fully from their apocalyptic transfiguration, and are only partially conscious of what Christ's victory over the world means here and now, having but a clouded view of the end to which it is leading. We see it all "as in a mirror."[77] Using the illustration of marriage, Jesus Christ illustrated the relationship that exists between the inauguration of his Kingdom here below, within the present make-up of the world, and its final accomplished form. Marriage is one of the corrupt institutions Christ has come to restore, in order to grant lasting fulfilment to the couple who allow themselves to be guided daily by him. But in the new order there will no longer be marriage,[78] or it will be completely different from what we know here below. But this does not preclude a close relationship between the renewal by Christ of marriage within temporal history and its fulfilment at the end of time. The radical newness of the Kingdom of God inaugurated by Christ is already transforming social structures within the temporal coordinates of history. This newness is illustrated by the incarnation of Christ, himself subject to the conditions of our historical and temporal situation. And this inauguration is a prefiguration of what the transfiguration of all things will be in the final fulfilment of the Kingdom. We are moving toward a future that has been guaranteed by the past and present action of Christ in the world. We are living in the time of signs and figures of what is to be. In the present progress of history we anticipate the definitive arrival of the Kingdom, this Kingdom which transfigures the present into an image of what will be tomorrow, this Kingdom which, though it will finally be posthistorical, is now fully historical, fully involved in temporality, but also marked with supertemporality, with a transhistoric dynamics.

(The passage of water to vapor can illustrate this historical continuity marked by a transforming discontinuity; or again the example used by Paul of grain that, by dying, becomes a new plant already prefigured in the seed and bound in with it long before developing into a new form.) [79]

The fundamental structure of humanity: its catholicity   Now the new calling addressed to all of humanity by God in Christ and the hidden power this new destiny exercises on it and on its development create among all men a fundamental unity, relativizing all their divisions and the specific characteristics of their diversity, making them purely accidental. The Word of God testifies to the unity of creation, and to the unity of all men in Christ.[80] The Word of God testifies that the reconciling work of God puts an end to all division and all enmity.[81]

Thus the calling of men in Christ makes ridiculous, but does not efface, all differences of race, nationality, language, culture, class, environment, confession and religion that could divide men. Christ reveals that the fundamental structure of humanity is its catholicity (its universality). And this catholicity of humanity, though it is not yet clearly perceived, in spite of all the secular signs of its realization (in technology, commerce, telecommunications, etc.), will become *fully manifest* in the last days. The Churches have become more conscious of the depths of this unity and of its dynamic function in history, in time, with an outlook on eternity. For it is in this world that God makes catholicity accessible to men by the ministry of Christ in his Church. Christ's purpose is to bring men of all times, all races, all places, and all conditions into an organic, living unity in Christ by the Holy Spirit, under the universal Fatherhood of God. This unity is not purely external. It is of a deeper dimension, more interior, well expressed by the term "catholicity." Catholicity reaches its fulness when what God has already begun in history is finally unveiled and fulfilled.[82] By proclaiming the necessity of openly realizing this fundamental unity of humanity, the Church has consciously expressed one of man's deepest tendencies. Thus it speaks to their highest aspirations and suffers to see them unsatisfied; it wants to help them reach their full development. That is why it offers them what it possesses inherently: a global perspective on man and human realities.[83]

The reconciliation of races   The catholicity of humanity is therefore a radical and fundamental contradiction of any theoretical or practical form of racism. Racism, as the Churches have declared, is a blatant denial of the Christian faith. (1) It denies the effectiveness of the reconciling work of Jesus Christ, through whose love all human diversities lose their divisive significance. (2) It denies our common humanity in creation and our belief that all men are made in the image of God. (3) It falsely asserts that it is our racial identity that gives meaning to our existence rather than Jesus Christ.[84]

The reconciliation of nations and of classes   This catholicity of the human family also invalidates any nationalistic, social or political ideology that would artificially divide humanity into hostile groups. The Word of God testifies that the reconciliatory work of God puts an end to all division and to all hate. This calling spurs us on to try to open, and keep open, the lines of communication between races, age groups, states and blocks of states, so as to promote reconciliation.[85] It is not a question of denying differences or struggles on the level of classes, nations or groups of nations in existence today. But we must eradicate the conditions that make them possible, for they are *already* condemned.

Unity does not do away with diversity; rather the opposite is true. It is true that diversity can be a perversion of catholicity. But it is also, and frequently, its authentic expression.[86]

A ceaseless combat for unity among men   However, the catholicity of humanity, as is true of all the characteristics granted it of Christ, does not belong to it of its own right. It is a gift that demands constant giving and constant receiving. It is the result of a permanent struggle, of the struggle Christ himself is carrying out in the world in order to attain a unity that is forever hampered by the forces of division at work in the world. This means that even unity has a polemical nature. It is the fruit of a ceaseless combat undertaken by Christ and carried on by men. In this case also, the cross is the only road that leads to resurrection.[87] This means that, patterning on the way opened by Christ, unity can be obtained only through a persevering struggle, accompanied by suffering and sacrifice.

An unwearying battle for development   This battle is for the development of a humanity called to forge its unity. The deepest motivating forces in history may be seen in the double event of the cross and the resurrection. By this judgment and this new beginning, God calls all men to associate with him in struggling against the evil he has condemned, and in favor of the renewal and development he has begun for mankind. Let us remember that the biblical witnesses see history as the battle-field where God and the powers of sin and destruction meet head on. They see God triumphing over resistance and promising the victory of grace and life over sin and death. Working from this center and from this perspective, the biblical witnesses look back at the past and consider the history of Israel as a continual struggle between the God of the covenant and his rebellious people.[88] They know that, though the history of nations is subject to the consequences of sin[89] and to the "elements of the world,"[90] God nonetheless rules by his patience.[91] And these witnesses look toward the future and contemplate future events. There they see the continually widening and intensifying development of the mystery of the cross and the resurrection. They can pick out the battle waged by the Spirit's power against the powers of darkness and the final victory of Christ's Kingdom.[92]

This is why humanity's march toward unity under the direction of Christ is a march and a combat in favor of the complete development of humanity. It demands the renewal of every culture, of all civilization. Indeed, this development cannot simply be reduced to economic growth. In order to be authentic, it must be complete, must foster every man and the whole man. "We cannot allow economics to be separated from human realities, nor development from the civilization in which it takes place. What counts for us is man — each individual man, each human group, and humanity as a whole."[93] It is a question, then, of a continuous quest for a new humanism,[94] for a full-fledged humanism that can ensure the full development of the whole man and of every man.[95]

Now the Christian Church has a primary role in the constant struggle Christ is carrying on in the world for the unity and full development of mankind.

A struggle in common with all men   By thus participating

directly in Christ's invisible action in the world, in his combat for unity and development, the Churches can rediscover just how much their mission conforms to the secret aspirations and essential destiny of the world. In certain ecclesiastical circles there has been much discussion of the hostility said to exist between the Church of Jesus Christ and the world. This hostility is real. But, from the perspective of Christ's victorious combat for the salvation of the world, this hostility is only accidental, neither essential nor fundamental. The Church is in fact only the tip of the iceberg as far as the structure and fundamental nature of humanity and nature are concerned. By allowing itself to be renewed by the "refreshing newness" of the living Christ, the Church puts the Christian in and with the world rather than over against it.[96] So it is necessary to emphasize strongly that the Church is the place from which one can see, quite often precariously it is true, what Christ is carrying out in permanent fashion in the world and for the world. The place where this action is taking place is throughout the whole world. For Christ is also carrying on his work of unity and development outside of the Church, throughout the world, at all moments of history — often without the Church being aware of it. For God is offering to all men the gift of renewal in their liberty. The Spirit's activity never constrains them, but it does open before them the doors of God's love and gives them the ability to participate in his creative, redemptive work.[97] That is why we can see God's work in history both in and through Jesus Christ and his Church, and in the world that seems to be, or for the time being is, outside the Church.[98] And this is also why we must work together (personally as members of society and as a Church) and why our effort can and must be common action. We are convinced that God is at work in the development that is presently taking place,[99] that he is summoning us to work with him, to work with one another, to work with all men who are involved in this work, whatever their convictions may be.[100]

In the Church and outside the Church   Since Christ's combat for the unity and development of humanity is taking place both within the Church and outside, and since any act contributing to this unity and development is an exterior sign of man's effective participation in this gigantic ongoing work of

Christ, we deduce that any combat entered upon by men for justice and liberty, when this justice and liberty are truly an expression of those we know in Christ, is a contribution to the genuine restoration of human unity and development in Christ. We must, the Churches tell us, consider that the realization of greater justice, liberty and dignity is part of the restoration of a genuine humanity in Christ. This calls for a more open and humble partnership with all who work for these goals, even if they do not share the same assumptions as we.[101] It is thus necessary to discern within current events the recurring signs of Christ's combat for the unity and renewal of humanity as they appear in the many changes taking place in the secular world.[102] And we also know (we will touch on this point again) that it is often by Christ's hidden work in the world, by political, economic and social changes, that the Lord is awakening his Church and forcing it to renew and transform, against its own tendency to spiritual drowsiness and static conservatism. This permanent renewal, this unceasing combat waged by Christ for the righting of all creation, takes on many different aspects. Besides these general cultural, spiritual, intellectual and artistic instances, it also takes on economic, political and ecclesiastical forms. Let us now look at these ecclesiastical aspects.

Three: the church's mandate and its renewal

We have said that man's calling, what permits him truly to be a man and fully to realize his humanity, is to become responsible, that is, one who puts his whole life, intellectual, spiritual, physical, material, cultural, economic, social and political, to work in fulfilling the plan of development mapped out by the Creator and Redeemer. We have also pointed out man's inability to respond fully to this invitation and to carry out its plan. But Christ, the New Man restored and re-created in the image of God, produces in man by the action of the Holy Spirit a new willingness to carry out his calling. He calls him again, invites him to participate with him in the renewal of all creation and of the cultural, social, economic and political life of humanity, according to the variety of civilizations and cultures through which God enriches humanity. Within this humanity in search of its calling and unable to realize it, Christians, who have discovered in Christ the perfect accomplishment of a full-fledged humanism in accord with God's plan and are thus assembled by Christ himself into a provisional community, make up an adumbration of the new humanity, a first form of its realization, while awaiting its full realization in the fulness of time. In Christ the new reconciled creation has already dawned; the Church lives in this certainty and presses on toward this hope.[1]

A. THE CHURCH, FIRST FORM OF THE NEW WORLD

But the Church is not something foreign to the world; it cannot form a community independent of the humanity surrounding it. It lives in the world for its Savior, but it lives with this world, sharing with it its deformations, its denials, its determinations and its historical pressures. It also shares with it the renewal of the cultural, social, political and economic life that Christ has undertaken, unbeknown to it. By their very nature, the members of the Church are united to this currently re-

prieved world which was condemned at Golgotha and which will be judged at the last day. But, in Christ and by his Holy Spirit, they belong to a community that was renewed at Pentecost and which will be transfigured at the glorious advent of the Lord. The mystery of faith is the mystery of the Church's incorporation into the New Man, Christ, and the mystery of this Church's involvement in the renewal of humanity whose destiny it shares. The liturgy is a renewal of the consecration of all human existence to the service of all men in order that God might be all in all. By its mission to the world, the Church renders testimony to the world of the origin and nature of the world's renewal, and is itself renewed in the renewal Christ grants to the world. It is only in the fulness of a transformed and renewed humanity that it can experience the fulness of the Holy Spirit's gifts.[2]

The faithful Church is, therefore, one that recognizes in Christ the motivating power behind the global development of humanity and receives from him the power to become in the world the pole on which this global development is centered, although it has no monopoly on it. For Christ has already undertaken this development throughout the world, and he is counting on the Church to reveal his hidden work in all its originality and, when he appears in his cosmic transfiguration, in all its fulness. At the end, after the last judgment, when everything that opposed this development will be destroyed from the world and from the Church, at the new creation, the world and the Church will be identical. For the Book of Revelation teaches us that the world will become the Church and that the Church's outer distinctive features will disappear, whereas the nations will blossom in the riches of their diversity and in their complementary solidarity and catholicity (universalism).[3]

The Church, source of development   The Church's rediscovery of Christ's work of re-creation and renewal for the world therefore includes on its part a new involvement in this work of general renewal of humanity. Far from separating it from the world,[4] the rediscovery of that complete mission which constitutes its originality and specificity turns it into the conscience of humanity, a community of involved individuals, responsible for the work of development and com-

plete renewal. And just as God's action and intervention in man's life do not eliminate, but rather establish, human responsibility, liberty and autonomy, so the faithful Church, by discovering Christ's renewing work in and for the world, does not give in to some religious fatalism or irresponsible providentialism, but on the contrary responds with all its might to its calling, to the calling of humanity. It participates actively, totally free and responsible, in the work of development and complete renewal of all humanity. And whereas all alienating forms of religion have a braking effect on the genuine, autonomous development of man and society, the response of the Church to Christ's renewing work makes up the sturdiest possible base and the most active source for the harmonious and integral development of humanity.

We also saw that man's discovery of his new calling, as it is addressed to him by Christ, the New Man, entails a complete transformation of his old nature, a fundamental renewal enabling him to rediscover his true nature, his true humanity. And this transformation, this "conversion" (*metanoia*), makes up a complete upheaval of his entire life, a fundamental transformation of his conceptions and behavior. And the same is true of the Church's renewal and of its community life. It is expressed by the continual renewal and transformation of the conceptions and practices current in the world and by a discovery of those conceptions and practices which are in accord with the newness of the New Man and his Kingdom.

The Church, seedbed of social transformation   Since man has been renewed in Christ, it is in the name of this particular renewal (and not in the name of some secular or religious ideology) that the Church must judge and recognize the work of social restoration that Christ is carrying out in the world. And it is in the name of this same truth, this same event, that it must judge and repudiate the tragic deformations of humanity that take place in the existence of men and within its own circles.

That constant renewal which characterizes the existence of the Church, when it is faithful to the orders of the Holy Spirit, appears in the local community just as well as in larger institutions. It expresses itself in a visible way by a modification of the conceptions and practices of each believer with respect

to the events that occur in his environment. It is at the level of the local community, for example, that any human exclusiveness of a racial or social order must be sought out and rooted up. It is there that the struggle against all forms of degradation and of economic, political and social exploitation of men must begin. It is also at this level that the identification and analysis of the causes of this degeneration must be undertaken, as well as the process of eliminating them.[5] The result can be that the decision that marks this renewal of the Christian community and its members may not always appear immediately as a purely religious choice. The new birth, that is, repentance and conversion, entails a repudiation of all forms of human degradation, on the level of individuals, politics, economics and society, and the decisions to act that now flow in a different direction. It implies a certain break with conceptual traditions and the habits of one's surroundings, a critical attitude toward local conformity be it social or political. In a word, death to oneself, a new life, in both the individual responding to his calling and the community of believers on the path of sanctification, implies a new social and political behavior. Christians who live by faith are ever torn anew from the limited and perverted life of the "old man" and from their natural sociological environment in order to put on the New Man. And this ongoing conversion is always expressed in concrete terms by a real change of attitude toward human relations, in politics and society. There is no conversion to God that does not lead one to consider his neighbor in a new light. The new life, by breaking racial, national and religious barriers, and all others that divide humanity, liberates man for community existence.[6]

The life of the Church, when it is directed by the renewing action of the Holy Spirit, is therefore made manifest in a continual renewal of all human relationships. In it the New Man makes his Kingdom manifest here below. This life in the Church includes, then, both a renewal of individual relationships between Christians within the community and the participation of this community and of each of its members in the greater combat Christ is waging on the outside for the renewal of society and the world.

The Church, first-fruits of human catholicity　　In order to

assure unity, the renewal and development of humanity, God in Christ is calling his Church, urging it to action. That is why he wants it to be catholic in nature, that is, universal; universal quantitatively, geographically, as well as qualitatively, entering into every area of man's life and activity.

A specific catholicity   The catholicity of the church must not be understood superficially. It consists not only of a new kind of relationship between men, nations, classes and races as such, but a vision of this relationship in connection with the God-head. Without this, catholicity could easily be mistaken for a pan-humanism, such as the twentieth century is insistently offering us with its purely secular understanding of inter-national society and of universal technology. This catholicity also takes in the future of the Church and of humanity, both in the end of time and in the present temporal state. It makes the future fulfilment of all things part of our time, a present reality giving meaning to every thing and every act. This is also what makes it impossible to confuse this catholicity in time and space, the goal of all human existence, with futuristic utopian goals proposed as a secular goal for human existence and society.[7] Such confusions cannot always be avoided for those outside the faith. For the external manifestations of the Church's catholic nature do not always appear, to the vision of a scientific phenomenological analysis for example, to be any different from other sociological phenomena of global inte-gration.

This catholicity is also rich and alive, offering to men the freedom to make richly manifest the multiple facets of their pluralistic nature. For multiplicity, variety and diversity are gifts of the Holy Spirit. Catholicity in Christ is, therefore, a pluralistic catholicity, requiring a unifying unity within the differentiated plurality of gifts and vocations: unifying in diversification and diversifying in unification. It is important, then, for the Church, while seeking unity, to provide a witness by the presence of this diversifying unification within its own life and to proclaim to the world the necessity of a cultural, social and political pluralism respectful of the complementary nature of human resources.[8]

A pluralism respectful of diversity   This diversity, however,

in no way justifies the delays Christians have caused in the formal accomplishment of the unity of the Church while the world is already carrying out in several areas a universality that, in spite of its partial nature, is nonetheless authentic in several respects. We must therefore pay special attention to ensure that our ecclesiastical catholicity not remain shy of the superficial catholicity of the world. We must be aware that this essential catholicity can become of little importance and even ridiculous to the world if it gives an abusive priority to confessional and ecclesiastical concerns. Also, we must affirm that the holiness of the Church[9] operates in the areas of economics, society and politics and that it is precisely in these areas that its catholicity appears. Too often the Church, in spite of all its declarations and sermons on unity, provides the sad spectacle of flagrantly denying its catholicity by allowing the divisions and creeping death of confessionalism, racism, nationalism, social injustice, cruel economic inequities, etc., to enter its ranks.[10] Is it not true that Churches have a tendency to submit endlessly to national needs and to accord to them greater value than to the requirements of catholicity? Is it not in fact true that they usually treat their supranationality, itself already realized by their communion in Christ, as practically ineffectual on their national political allegiances, especially in the case of conflict between two nations or groups of nations?

Catholicity realized in holiness   For all these reasons the Church must allow itself to be renewed, tested, constantly visited by the renewing Word of God, must pray to receive from the Holy Spirit its true renewal. For its holiness is an aspect of its catholicity and is the condition on which its credibility, the "believability" of its witness to the world, is based. It cannot fulfil its mission, cannot truly become apostolic as the world so greatly needs in order to understand itself and the meaning of its calling and future, without the renewing power of holiness, without sanctification.[11]

In order properly to address a message to the world, then, the Church must allow itself to undergo constant purification. It must ever be looking for what separates it from Christ. It must track down within itself those misunderstandings which so often cause conflict, those deceitful myths about others which

are so easily colporteured about by social and political ideologies and by clans with opposing interests. It must become aware of the nature of these divergent interests which are at the beginning of so many conflicts.[12]

The Church, where political awareness comes about   The Church can recognize the external forces at work within it and on it, and can get rid of them, only by means of precise sociological analysis. It alone is able to resolve dispassionately debates that too often are based only on suspicions or intentions. In particular, it must discover and analyze all forms of violence in the world and in itself, be it locally, nationally, regionally or globally. It must above all denounce all forms of violence that are hidden or more or less openly admitted but which no one dares denounce because they are carried out under the umbrella of law and order, while that very law and order permits unjust, injurious privileges, harmful to individuals and social or racial groups.[13] It must denounce not only all forms of active violence, but also inaction, passive conformity, political indifference or anti-reformist conservatism that allows violent situations to emerge or continue.[14]

It can, therefore, face social and political contradictions only if it is so rooted in Christ that the inevitable divisions that separate men on questions of analysis and political involvement appear to its members to be secondary when compared to the faith that unites them. It is only on this condition that oppositions may be robbed of their ideological virulence.

The originality and unique specificity of the Church's catholicity require it not to be identified with any existing political or social order on the pretext that it is the expression of God's will, nor with any revolutionary project on the pretext that it is the expression of divine judgment pronounced against an unjust order of things or that it is at last providing humanity with the order it has so long desired. The only valid acknowledgment it can make of any system present or future is to state clearly that the present order is only a provisional stage in history, that it is perfectible and reformable, that it has no definitive value, that it is not of a religious or sacred character,[15] and that it can in no case be identified with the full will of God as expressed in the appearance of his Kingdom.

The tremendous difficulty the Churches face in the political problems that must inevitably divide men resides in the fact that they have not expended enough effort in educating their members to take these divergences as a matter of dialectics and secondary to the unity of faith. Their faith is not an adult faith. They are not prepared to recognize that the Kingdom of God manifest in Christ is, *in daily reality,* more important and more demanding than temporal politics and that it is in fact what orders politics. Nor have they been sufficiently trained to put their political options through the sieve of obedience to Christ. All forms of social or political order and the institutions that give them their individual shapes must be open to the rediscovery of new human values and receptive to the needs for change inherent in service for justice and peace. Because of the pressure of today's revolutionary forces, in science, technology, society, politics and religion, we are witnesses of a period of tumultuous transformation requiring structures capable of rapid adaptation to new conditions and even ready to try to stay a step ahead of genuine new needs as they arise.[16]

The Church, source of reconciliation   It is, therefore, in this world, already divided by a multitude of interests, by ideologies, by factors of race, society and nationalism, that God is interposing his power in order to provide men with access to reconciliation, unity and love, that is, to catholicity and humanity, by the ministry of Christ.[17]

The Church is a prefiguration of the new human community: renewed to the extent that it allows Christ to work out in it reconciliation and love between those who are different by race, social class, age, religious or political conditions,[18] and to the extent that it allows itself to become involved by Christ in the struggle for reconciliation and unity among men.

The Church, both the local community and the universal Church, is called to join with men in bearing the sufferings that crush them down and in overcoming those divisions which destroy them. It is beside them, sharing the groans of a creation awaiting deliverance.[19]

The Church is not a goal in itself   Nor must the Church turn in on itself and become self-authenticating. For that reconciliation which can unite men divided by race, self-interest, ideologies and national allegiances can never come about in a vacuum. Reconciliation can be genuine only if those who experience it participate in practical action and in the concrete struggle Christ has undertaken in the world in order to carry out around the Church this very reconciliation. For the Church can find internal unity — a unity that is not artificial and hypocritical — only by struggling on the outside for the unity of mankind and by becoming involved, by an active solidarity, in the work of those who today are endeavoring to bring men closer and closer. It is, moreover, in this outside involvement that it will be able to abandon the petty preoccupations that so often paralyze the resolution of its internal quarrels. The Spirit who unites us in the Church also makes us more conscious of the world's needs — we can no longer stay on the side content with observing the strife and tumult of our age. The Holy Spirit is inviting us to share the infinite love of Christ with others. And thus he requires us to accept his condemnation of our fears and betrayals and, by love for him, to endure if necessary shame, oppression and apparent defeat. The world is the place where God is at work to make everything new and that is where he exhorts us to work with him.[20]

The Church, a source of action in the world   The Church, then, is a place where men may prepare and, by responding to their calling as men, become involved in the struggle for unity and the development of humanity. The Church is indeed under perpetual orders to come out of the world in order to be sent into the world. This double movement is the basis of dynamic catholicity. Each of these two movements requires different words and different acts according to different situations, but always the two movements belong together. The constitutive center of this double movement is corporate worship in which Christ himself is the one who both calls and sends.[21] Worship that does not include this double movement — into the sanctuary and out into the world — is not genuine (or reasonable) worship.[22] Opposition between "religious" persons who expect worship to take them out of the world and "political" or "pragmatic" beings who expect worship to give them their marching orders, is a false opposition. In order to be faithful to its specific mission, the Church must maintain the tension between these two poles to an intense degree, and must respond simultaneously to this double requirement.

B. THE CHURCH, CRITICAL CONSCIENCE OF SOCIETY

The Church's mission, then, is not that of leading people to itself. Its task is on the contrary to prepare them (by bringing them together for this preparation) to participate with others in the global renewal of society in view of the new world. Its goal is the realization of an authentic humanity that it prefigures and founds in Christ by the double testimony of its words and its acts, and in particular by the services the Holy Spirit incites it to furnish.[23]

The Church, bearer of the critical Gospel   We have seen that the prodigious powers given by Christ to men for the exploitation of creation and the harmonious development of society are powers that man is forever degrading and transforming into forces of destruction and oppression. The great task of the Church is nothing less than the restoration of these powers, both by proclaiming their intended purpose wherever they are exercised and by searching out the means capable of working toward mastering them and subjecting them to the goals for which they were granted. This means that the Church's function is essentially one of criticism, in the most positive and elevated sense of this term, since the Gospel it proclaims by its acts and words is essentially a critical Gospel, bearing both God's judgment and condemnation and his redemptive grace.

For we have also seen that the techniques and powers at man's disposal are neither good nor bad in themselves. They are only means to accomplish God's will, but means that, once usurped by sinful men, can always be used for devious purposes.[24] The Church is, as it were, the protesting conscience of society, charged with safeguarding the legitimate goals of this society and with protecting the endangered men who make it up.[25] Its critical mission is therefore essential for the conservation and harmonious development of society. If it does not carry out this specific ministry, the Church loses its meaning and becomes a dead, static element in society, participating in its destruction. It contributes to it either by multiplying the number of its purely religious activities which give it the appearance of life but which often lead to flight away from the world, or, on the contrary, by politicizing or secularizing its activities to such an extent that it no longer indicates to the world the unique source and goal, irreplaceable, suprapolitical and suprasocial, of every form of politics and every social arrangement.

The Church, sentinel for humanity   In the perpetual ambiguity of social forces at work in all societies, in the permanent struggle of Christ for the restoration of the world, in the eternal promiscuity of Good Friday and Easter, it is impossible for men who are ignorant of this key to history to discern what is right and good according to God. It is therefore the Church's task to point it out. But the discernment it needs for this task is not an automatic gift. It is never a natural thing for any Christian to join in the struggle Christ is fighting every day for the salvation of the world because, in this struggle, no one can ever take refuge in any form of neutrality. We all undergo the contradictory forces that are at work in the world, and the discernment necessary to apprehend its nature can be received only by faith, faithfulness and obedience. This discernment is the fruit of the basic spiritual exercise of ecclesiastical life called sanctification, that is, renewal in Christ by prayer, meditation on the Word of God, and action. Christians, therefore, can discern together, communally, ecclesiastically, the signs of the times and the nature of the social and political forces at work in the world only by these same spiritual exercises carried on in common: political discernment is an aspect of sanctification. And the prophetic ministry of the Church, when it is exercised collegially, is a consequence of its sanctification in community.

The necessary criticism of powers   Wherever that power is exercised is the Church's mission field. For this is where men's struggles and intrigues to take over these powers and dominate others occur. Broadcasting technology, for example, can be used either as a powerful means of communication or as a deceitful means of manipulation. All the centers of power — governments, commercial centers, industry, the military, labor unions, political parties and the Churches themselves — should be called to account for the use they make of their powers. And this examination must forever place them face to face with their reason for being in the world, to see if they are faithful servants.[26] In intellectual centers, the places of higher learning and research that to a large extent determine the forms of tomorrow's life and society, where a worldwide society is now emerging, it is important for the testimony of Christians to be present in order to make known the Lord's purposes for this civilization.[27] Rapidly developing urban centers, suburbs, and rural areas demand from the Church a missionary action intended to dissipate social prejudice, discriminatory and oppressive practices that paralyze the development and expansion of developing human groups. This mission must also be carried out in centers of decision and public opinion capable of influencing relations between developed and developing countries, and it must effect a new international missionary strategy reflecting Christ's goals for universal development and for unified management of creation.[28]

The Church must prepare for its role as critic   The Church, then, has innumerable opportunities for intervention, for the exercise of its role as critic. Its duty is to use a lucid analysis to determine priorities, and to choose its structures and investments in terms of its primary missionary tasks.

It is important to emphasize that the participation of the Church in the universalizing renewal Christ is bringing about throughout the world begins with that combat which submits the Church itself to the critical examination of the Gospel. This combat perforce involves it, first of all, in that social struggle which must begin on the community level.[29] But the local community has an obligation itself to participate in the struggles in which the Church as a whole is involved on the national, regional and global levels. For such involvement requires the fraternal worship, discipline and correction of a universal community. Such an outlook implies the complete renewal of interchurch and interconfessional relationships and of ecclesiastical structure.[30]

More collaboration with the outside   The renewed Churches must also, locally as well as nationally, regionally and globally, break with the tradition of confessional institutions and resolutely undertake a program of greater and more frankly stated collaboration not only with Christians of other denominations but also with all who are ready to work toward the same practical goals even when they do not share the same assumptions.[31] The Churches must agree to recognize more openly and more freely the diversity of the Spirit's gifts within and outside of the Church.

A continual revitalization from within   Finally, in all these actions, which are only some of the forms of active testimony, the Church must never lose sight of what makes up the center of its testimony: a constant rediscovery and worship of the New Man, of him who is the source, the beginning and the end of the development and unity of man and creation. He it is who communicates to those who join his service the glorious liberty of participating in all forms of liberation and emancipation that permit the complete development of the human being and society.

C. FAILURE AND TRIUMPH OF THE NEW HUMANITY

We have dwelt enough on the various forms of degradation into which politics, society and economics have slid. We must now recognize that the Church, in spite of the promises and means of renewal granted to it to enable man to receive his calling anew and to accomplish his humanity by rebuilding social relationships and returning the ruling powers to the purposes they were meant to fulfil, can also be party to a denial of vocation and to halting its fulfilment. In order for it to be forgiven and renewed, it must take cognizance of its inclination to join others in destroying what God has built.

Christians have too easily adopted a false and dishonest image of the Church — false and dishonest both from the point of view of fundamental theology and from the point of view of history. According to this conception, the world around the Church is where evil reigns, while the Church is floating in the sea of evil as the one place where good may clearly be seen at work. This view is false and dishonest in two directions: on the one hand, it belittles the continual work of renewal, development and unity God has undertaken through Christ in the world, but unbeknown to it, continually fostering the

reformation of structures and of the social and political practices of humanity. On the other hand, it neglects the facility
with which Christians as individuals, but also the Church as
a corporation, become corrupted by the very same demons
that seduce the world: economic and financial selfishness,
racism, nationalism, etc.

What lends grandeur and novelty to the contemporary
ecumenical documents is that they recognize with perfect
lucidity the Church's propensity to become contaminated by all
those forms of degradation which are rampant in the world.
And they denounce unequivocally the cause of this unfaithfulness: the Churches' neglect to take the Gospel seriously as the
source of all life, and therefore their conformity to social, economic and political pressure by prestige groups or by extremely
ambitious groups (such as, for example, certain revolutionary
movements). Or it can take the form of conformity by complicity when a Church transforms cowardice into virtue and
justifies forms of destruction or conservatism, of nationalism,
militarism, racism or revolution, in religious terms. Or it can
do so unconsciously when social inertia gives a Church a certain
spirituality (by suggesting that it has no need of worrying
about the temporal order) and thus makes it the passive
accomplice of the hate, rivalry, division, injustice, war and
crime of society. What is behind all this, let us remember, is
the Church's abandonment of the authority of the universal
critical Gospel, and especially the abandonment of him to
whom this Gospel bears witness. It thus becomes a more or
less conscious submission, abandonment to an ideology.

1. *The Churches' Necessary Confession of Guilt*

The Churches must therefore confess their guilt in the world's
decay. This confession is in fact a condition of their reconver-
sion and renewal.

In the ecumenical texts to which we are referring, the
Churches have courageously undertaken such a confession.
They first recognize that the individual Christian's vulnera-
bility to the forces of evil makes the entire Church very fragile.
Man has been renewed in Christ, they proclaim, and it is in
the light of this truth that we must judge and repudiate the
tragic deformations of humanity in human existence. But some

of these deformations may be found within the Christian community.[32]

Racism in the Church   One example of this contamination is racism. In spite of all the sermons against racism, the practice of racial segregation may still be found within the Church, so that even when they gather in Christ's name some are excluded on account of their color. Such a denial of catholicity demands the speediest and most passionate rejection. Renewal must begin in the local community, by detecting and dethroning all exclusiveness of race and class and by fighting all economic, political and social degradation and exploitation of men.[33]

The Church, accomplice of nationalistic, economic and ideological conflicts   But racism is not the only example. In the cruel arena of contemporary history — and very often among Church members — we may observe demonic forces struggling against the rights and liberties of man. Conflicts between races and nations tear apart the fabric of our common life, as developed and developing countries become more and more alienated from each other, and ideologies and crusades clash in daily struggle for survival.[34] All these divisions are found, barely reduced, within the Church, and they destroy its unity and catholicity. Evil does not rage only within the hearts of individuals. It affects institutions, especially ecclesiastical institutions.[35]

The conservative laziness of the Church   Although the world is steadily changing, we know that the Church as organization, both clergy and laymen, is too slow to change and too ready to resist change. We know that in the developed countries the Churches themselves are not necessarily very developed, and that the Churches of the developing countries are not necessarily underdeveloped.[36]

The great sin of the Church: lack of conscience   One of the great discoveries of today's Churches is their own lack of conscience and awareness of the nature of the conflicts that are raging in the world and their inability to search out and understand the objective causes of these conflicts. The result of this deficiency is to limit their means of acting and intervening since they are too easily content with almsgiving and superficial remedies. Historically speaking, the expansion of Christianity, often propagated at the price of tremendous efforts, has led to an increased appreciation of human dignity. But today God can judge us in our world with all its possibilities. And, particularly, he can judge us, Christians in the rich West, because we have been content with handing out charity to those in need and because we have not helped men find the well-being and dignity that could be theirs. This is true even within the richest countries.

The abdication of the laity   This resistance by ecclesiastical institutions to change and to necessary adaption is well known. It is often a pretext used by laymen not to take up their full responsibilities in the renewal of the temporal order. But it is their duty to use their own initiative and take action without waiting passively for directives and precepts from others. They must try to infuse a Christian spirit into people's mental outlook and daily behavior, into the laws and structures of the civil community.[37]

An active minority would be sufficient   Christians have many more possibilities to act than they realize. Only their collective inertia keeps them from seizing the initiative and producing the necessary effect. This could easily be attained through effort. The present conviction among parliamentarians — that the body politic cares neither for progress nor for justice — can be shaken if only ten to fifteen percent of the electorate, a potential swing vote, show sufficient tenacity. Vocal university protest in Britain, for instance, modified the government's intention to impose higher charges on foreign students. Hitherto, Christians in the developed world have not shown political leadership in the field of economic assistance, in spite of the fact that they alone, among the developed nations, could provide a ten percent dedicated minority in virtually every constituency.[38]

Shortsighted parochialism   The Churches and parishes are also unable to go beyond the level of local, regional or national concerns or to participate actively in the formation of a cooperative society that would go beyond these limits. Christians who know from their Scriptures that all men are created by God in his image and that Christ died for all should be in the forefront of the battle to overcome a provincial, narrow sense of solidarity and to create a sense of participation in a world-wide responsible society with justice for all.[39]

A deadly political and social conformity   What must be recognized by all observers as the cause of death among the Churches, their incapacity for self-renewal, their deaf ear to the commands of the Spirit, is their own place in the political and social status quo, their lack of dynamic reformation that could bring their lives and their societies into conformity to God's plan. For our hope is in him who makes all things new. He judges our structures of thought and actions and renders them obsolete. If our false security in the old and our fear of revolutionary change lead us to defend the status quo or to patch it up with half-hearted measures, we may all perish and, worse yet, may be the means of degradation and death for all men. The death of the old may cause pain to some, but our failure to build up a new world community may bring death to all. In their faith in the coming Kingdom of God and in their search for his righteousness, Christians are urged to participate in the struggle of millions of people for greater social justice and for world development.[40] This fear of change, this social and political conservatism so characteristic of the Churches, is denounced as one of the most typical signs of their spiritual drowsiness and disregard for men's fate. If the Church is not on the front line of change and renewal in the world in order to direct them and dominate them for the purpose of subjecting them to God's plan, it becomes responsible not only for its own sociological backwardness with respect to the evolution of the world, but also for distortion and confusion in these changes and, thereby, for all the political and social catastrophes of the world. The Word of God testifies that in Jesus Christ God makes the world new. But we Christians, who have often resisted change and progress through our anxiety or indifference, now see the acceleration of social and political change. We are called at the same time to critical examination and unhesitating involvement.[41]

Fear of change   This resistance to change so characteristic of the Church, and its resultant inability to orient change in the direction of God's plan for the world, originates in a fundamental deficiency of Church members: their own resistance to the Spirit's transforming and renewing word. Many are too satisfied with their comfortable heritage and too unwilling to respond to the legitimate requests of their brothers, their fellow-men. Many of us, all of us perhaps, live in fear of change. We are afraid of being disturbed, of losing what we have acquired, often unjustly and at the expense of others. More deeply, we fear the uncertainty of change, the unknown future and the unpredictability of circumstances. But change may bring about the fuller human opportunities we seek, and enable men to produce the wealth to meet the needs of all. As we work with others in the changing of outmoded structures and in the creation of new wealth, so we find our true humanity. We welcome this world of change in which we believe God is continually at work.[42]

Fear and irresponsibility provoke violence   Of course we know well that in this ambiguous world any change is ambivalent and is therefore not necessarily the bearer of progress. But what is serious in customary resistance to change is that it paralyzes the possibilities of progress and creates situations where injustice and violence may take root: the ominous, camouflaged violence of those who profit from injustice and who want to maintain it behind claims of order and legality, but also the inevitable growing violence of those who struggle against injustice in the name of a justice that is ambiguous but nonetheless promises possibilities of renewal. For where fear of reform and the power of special interests oppose change, not only does development appear impossible, but violence rears its head. It is the work of courageous, dynamic love to break through this resistance by reforming will and practice, and, where necessary, by nonviolent revolution.[43] The blind defense of political and religious institutions and the social conservatism by principle that obstructs the mutations of history are therefore perversions of the catholicity of the Church, of that profound catholicity by which it is re-created from within and renewed by the changing forms of history when these take the direction of their dynamic purpose received from Christ.[44]

An uncritical docility to change   It would be incorrect not to point out here another form of perversion in the Church: its uncritical conformity to the changes of the world. For it is clear that in the ambiguity of a history dominated by opposing forces every change is not necessarily a progressive change from Christ's viewpoint. It is therefore essential for the Church to be so renewed by the Spirit of Christ that it is able to discern the true nature of the changes brought about in the history and is thus able to deter those which are potentially destructive. The Church is faced by the twin demands of continuity in the one Holy Spirit, and renewal in response to the call of the Spirit amid the changes of human history.[45]

The Church is occasionally strongly tempted to adopt the easy solution of complete identification with the secularized forms of change as though such change were valid in its own right. The Church's identification with the revolutionary status quo of tomorrow, as though social and political revolution were self-authenticating and the bearer of God's future, is just as alienating for the Church and for the world as its identification with the status quo of today and yesterday, as though the existing social and political institutions and their economic practices necessarily expressed in themselves God's plan for the world.

The ambiguity of secular catholicity   There are innumerable forms of secular catholicity that make up double traps for the Church. These forms of catholicity are the ones being achieved by technology, uniting all men in a single, non-religious culture. This external, technological universalization of humanity is certainly a reason for hope, for it is a first sign of its true catholicity. It emphasizes strongly the fundamental truth that human nature is of one blood, that every man has the same rights and the same dignity, whatever his race or any other of his characteristics may be. It announces and proclaims the basic catholicity of humanity, founded not only on the fact that the one God has created all men in his image, but also on the work of Jesus Christ, who "for us men" became man and was crucified, and who constitutes the Church that is his body as a new community of new creatures.[46]

Secular society has been able to propose methods of conciliation and unification that often seem more effectual than the

Church's. Seen from outside, the Churches seem because of their divisions to be dangerously behind the world. They seem to be unconscious of the preparatory work carried out by Christ in the world, and they allow themselves to be turned away from this genuine work by their tedious preoccupation with their own concerns.[47] But these outward, incomplete forms of secular catholicity, useful anticipations of the Church's visible catholicity, provisional and superficial expressions of the promised catholicity of the world, can nevertheless be snares for the world and for the church. For the world, because the realization of secular catholicity can turn mankind from its true source of unity and from its genuine humanity in Christ. For the Churches, because they too often think that by simply associating their activity, effort, and even their temporal calling with the realization of secular, external and provisional forms of a catholicity understood in terms of technology, society, economics or politics, they are bringing about the true catholicity of Christ. But by making such a confusion and by forgetting to point out, beyond these necessary and provisional steps, the living Christ who is their beginning and end, they themselves err, and turn the world from the initial source of all true unity and all renewal, Jesus Christ.

The ambiguity of ecclesiastical power　　Another form of perversion for the Church is the lack of a critical attitude toward political, economic and social powers because it feels the need to submit to the state and to the temporal requirements of society. When it becomes too closely associated with these powers, the Church can itself become a degrading and alienating force.[48] No ecclesiastical power is exempt from this potential perversion. For all centers of power are ambiguous in nature, and men are engaged in an increasingly bitter struggle to gain control of these centers so as to attain the direction of society — a direction liable at any time to turn into exploitation.[49]

　　The Church is no more sheltered from tyranny by a man or group, by a minority or a majority, than is any other element of society.[50]

Complacency toward the rich and the powerful　　To avoid this kind of alteration, even prostitution, the Church must be ever alert to the different forms of inequality between the strong and the weak, the rich and the poor, both within the Church and in society as a whole. It must take up the cause of the poor and oppressed, without allowing its love to relinquish the role of positive critic toward all. By abandoning solidarity with the true poor (those who have no social power), the Church denies itself and distorts thereby the society of which it is a part. The Word of God teaches that Christ takes the side of the poor and oppressed. But we Christians do not always show our allegiance as he did. We now see a worldwide struggle for economic justice. We must work to vindicate the rights of the poor and oppressed and to establish economic justice among the nations and within each state.[51]

Desertion in conflict   The Church runs the same risk of perversion in regard to political conflict. The Church's too ready tendency is to join the strong side, the winning side, rather than to make an active attempt at reconciliation. The Word of God teaches that God, in Christ, established peace on earth. It teaches that the reconciling work of God can put an end to all division and hate. But we Christians, who have often lived in reciprocal hostility, allow ourselves to be overcome by worldly divisions, in the name of a misconceived solidarity. We have often been irreconcilable. We see that the nations are seeking means of co-existence in order to avoid a war of inconceivable repercussions. This is for us a call to a creative "pro-existence." It drives us to seek to open and to keep open the lines of communication between races, age groups, nations and blocs, in order to bring about reconciliation. To do so it must speak out where no one else dares to, or where truth is not respected, where human lives or human dignity are endangered, and where opportunities for a better future are neglected.[52]

This task is just as delicate in a reactionary or conservative atmosphere as in a revolutionary situation. For whenever the Church takes upon itself the fate of victims of an arbitrary society, that of crushed and scorned minorities, it seems to be selling out the social order, be it old or new, since it is defending the adversaries of that order. If it is faithful to its mission, it cannot avoid political slander from all segments of the society whose oppressed victims its adopts.

Complicity in social backwardness   The Churches have recognized that too often their teaching does not measure up to the needs of the situation. In today's worldwide community the individual's rights are preforce tied in with the struggle to raise the standard of living for the disenfranchised of all countries. The rights of man cannot be safeguarded in a world filled with blatant inequality and always at the mercy of social conflict. The Churches are duty-bound to make their members understand this, and they must give the example, in their own relationships, of respect, dignity and humane legality as well as liberty of opinion, even of publication. Too often such is not the case. The Churches often show a great indifference, also, for activities in favor of development, reconciliation and social progress. This is why they are unable to make governments understand that this type of service should be recognized and supported as ranking at least as highly as national service.[53]

Indifference toward real unity   The Churches also recognize that by the denial of their internal liberty, either on the local level (by more or less consciously accepting the discrimination of racism, social classes, generations, religious conviction or political affiliation[54]) or on the interconfessional level, they are only helping to deny the unity of humanity. The Church is, indeed, rather bold, or perhaps uncomprehending, in claiming to be the first sign of the future humanity when it is incapable of bringing about its own unity. However well founded such a claim may be, the world hears it sceptically, and its whole message of reconciliation thereby loses its credibility, its believableness.[55] It thus cripples the work of the Holy Spirit, which empowers the Church in its unity to be a ferment in society, for the renewal and unity of mankind.[56] Thus the Church transgresses doubly, against its own catholicity and against that of humanity, when, on the one hand, it lightly accepts ecclesiastical and confessional divisions on the local or global level and does not work at the eradication of these unity-destroying factors, and, on the other hand, when it tolerates without contest social, racial, national or economic divisions and antagonisms within itself or within the society where it operates. These two kinds of division are among the most important causes of loss of credibility for the Christian mes-

sage in the world.[57] The Church's mission to bring about reconciliation is paradoxical and often contradictory. For though
part of its task is to try to bring adversaries together, another
part is to struggle against the concrete injustices that cause the
adversaries to quarrel. And the two parties are usually not
willing to denounce these concrete forms of injustice when
they are profiting from them, nor to permit the Church to do
away with them.

Acceptance of false forms of unity   Too often the Churches
confuse the unity and catholicity of the Church with other
solidarities and communities based on such human societal
factors as race, nation, social or historical group, etc., which are
also factors of division and conflict. Examples of this confusion
occur whenever Christian communities

allow the Gospel to be obscured by prejudices that prevent
them from seeking unity;

allow their membership to be determined by discrimination based on race, wealth, social class or education (are
there not even Churches that require their members to be of
a certain nationality, or which grant members different
rights according to their nationality?) ;

do not exhibit in all the variety of their life together the
essential oneness in Christ of men and women;

allow cultural, ethnic or political allegiances to prevent the
organic union of Churches that confess the same faith within the same region;

prescribe their own customary practices as binding on other
Christians as the condition for cooperation and unity;

permit loyalty to their own nation to hinder or to destroy
their desire for mutual fellowship with Christians of another nation;

allow themselves to be forced into unity by the state for
nationalistic ends, or break their unity for political reasons.

It is by recognizing these confusions and by seeking to eliminate them that our Churches will be able to overcome the
forces that still keep us apart from each other.[58]

Ecclesiastical egocentricity   Any Church that does take into consideration its internal problems, spiritual and ecclesiastical, and which does not recognize that the external sociological divisions of its members have a destructive effect on its unity in Christ, is not capable of understanding the true nature of its catholicity and its mission in the world. The same is true of a purely Church-oriented ecumenism whose goals are reduced to the unity of Christians among themselves and which thus loses sight of the unity projected by Christ of all the members of the civil community, be it local, national or worldwide, and the solution of the human problems dividing them. These two levels of humanity may not be separated.

Complicity in the arms race   In this context, the participation of Christians in the arms race and the refusal of inert, inactive Churches, within their own nations and throughout the world, to paralyze this destructive power, are obvious forms of the internal perversion and spiritual prostitution that are rife within the Church. When so many people are hungry, when so many homes suffer misery, when so many men are steeped in ignorance, when so many schools, hospitals and suitable homes are yet to be built, any public or private waste, any ostentatious waste, national or individual, any debilitating arms race is an intolerable scandal. Our solemn duty is to denounce it.[59]

False realism and irresponsibility   The Church's shirking of responsibility in all these areas, often justified on a superficial level by a limited conception of realism or by fear of arousing hostility or division, is in fact a lack of true realism and spiritual discernment. It is a sign of irresponsibility.[60] For, in fact, divisions only multiply because of the ostensible neutrality or regular abstention of the Churches in the face of social and national conflicts and because of their cowardly refusal to take up the struggle for truth and justice.

Pious, frightened patter   In such circumstances the Church's witness, which was meant to express God's intervention in the world in favor of peace and justice, becomes useless, superficial patter. For when the Church speaks out honestly in God's name, its word is never insignificant. Rather, it is noticed, since it is spoken where no one else dares speak, where truth is scorned, where human life and dignity are endangered and where opportunities for a better future are neglected.[61] In the Church's witness the Word of God must be clearly distinguishable; it must not simply appear as the reflection of opinions predominant in the country or in the social and political strata occupied by present and prospective members. The Gospel must at all times be a critical Gospel, messenger of judgment and grace. It is never cheap or verbose.[62]

Words with no practical results   And so, as regards racism, nationalism, capitalism, collectivism, etc., the Church's statements and acts can be effective only if the constant preoccupation is one of bettering the economic and political situation of exploited groups.[63] In short, the Church inspires no confidence in what it says when it is incapable of incarnating the signs of the new humanity in itself or of recognizing these signs in the world where Christ is at work. And its faithfulness becomes completely suspect when its only preoccupation is with its own numerical and institutional strength,[64] or if it is content with denouncing rampant injustice elsewhere without the critical spirit or the courage to see and denounce what is happening at home.[65] The recognition of its complicity in all the forms of economic and social perversion is already a sign of the Church's renewal. For, since the Church can never reach the perfection of its Lord, it can hope to witness an expansion of its truth and love only if it is constantly renewed by recognizing and confessing its sins, by an active repentance capable of producing new acts and new decisions (a *praxis* consequent with its profession), a *metanoia,* that is, a conversion of acts.

2. *The Church Renewed by the Grace of Discernment*
   and the Courage of Repentance

The Church begins to recover a full awareness of its responsibility when, looking at the world and realizing the marvelous possibilities God grants man in his inventive genius, it takes upon itself the task, with all its ramifications and difficulties, of assuring the mastery of all these possibilities and providing direction for them consonant with God's plan. We live in a new world of exciting prospects. For the first time in history we can consider the unity of humanity as a reality. For the first time we know that all men could have their part in the world's resources if they were put to proper use. The new possibilities offered by technology make old dreams into realities. Because today we have knowledge about conditions throughout the earth, and the means to deal with them, we are without excuse. It is one world, and the gross inequalities between the people of different nations and different continents are as inexcusable as the gross inequalities within nations.[66]

The importance of simultaneous local and worldwide plans It is by the expansion of its local plan into a worldwide plan that the Church can repent for its narrowness, can no longer be content to act within restricted limits, and can assume its full responsibilities. Most men, including Christians, are aware of their responsibility for members of their own national communities who are in need. But few have discovered that we now live in a world in which people in need in all parts of the world are our neighbors for whom we bear responsibility. Christians who know from their Scriptures that all men are created by God in his image and that Christ died for all, should be in the forefront of the battle to overcome a provincial, narrow sense of solidarity and to create a sense of participation in a worldwide responsible society with justice for all.[67]

The collective responsibility of Christians for development and disarmament   As its vision expands, the Church must confess its responsibility toward the world's suffering. In spite of the fact that science and technology have for the first time vanquished the distances of space and time and placed superabundant and growing wealth at man's disposal, eighty percent of this community's resources are at the disposal of only twenty percent of the world's people, living in the main around the North Atlantic. And while one segment of humanity is rich and growing higher, the rest still struggle in varying degrees of poverty and have little certainty of breaking out of their stagnation in the next decades. Now the majority of Christians live in the developed North, and since this area is wealthy far beyond the general level of world society, they profit from this unbalanced prosperity and must in conscience account for their stewardship. Moreover, all Christians bear heavy responsibility for a world in which it can seem "normal" to spend billions of dollars per year on armaments, yet difficult to mobilize more than ten billion dollars for the works of economic and social cooperation.[68]

A call to an objectively motivated repentance   This is why it is the Church's responsibility to proclaim that, faced with these inequalities, injustices and aberrations, the peoples of the earth must repent and change their mentality and behavior. The Church's calling is to work for the establishment of a worldwide society and to call men and nations to repentance.[69] To be complacent in the face of the world's need is to be guilty of practical heresy.[70]

This conversion, the result of repentance, leads immediately to a practical ecumenism and a shared vision of the Church's action and of the world's. As we try to meet the challenge, we recognize the importance of cooperating at every level with the Roman Catholic Church, with other nonmember Churches, with nonchurch organizations, adherents of other religions, men of no religion, indeed with men of goodwill everywhere.[71]

Conversion: behavior and structures transformed for action The repentance of the Church is expressed by its conversion, that is, by its continual renewal and its willingness to modify its behavior as well as its structures and organization. Thus it can continually adapt to the new tasks repentance itself presents. Mobilizing the people of God for mission today means releasing them from structures that inhibit them in the Church and enabling them to open out in much more flexible ways to the world in which they live. This necessitates:

1. A continuing re-examination of the structures of Church life at all levels, i.e., the local parish, the denominational synods and conferences and their agencies, the councils of Churches at national, regional and world levels. All these must ask, not "Have we the right structures for mission?", but "Are we totally structured for mission?"

2. A re-examination of the variety of tasks to which the people are called in their ministry of the world. Laymen and laywomen express their full commitment to mission, not primarily through the service they give within the Church struc-

tures, but pre-eminently through the ways in which they use their professional skills and competence in their daily work and public service. We need to employ all the gifts God has given to his people — whether they be gifts of proclamation, healing, political activity, administration, running a home, etc. We need to explore how, in the diverse roles in which we find ourselves, we can creatively and with integrity express our full humanity — whether it be as young people, or women, or members of minority groups, or people in positions of authority, etc. In all these, we need to recognize what is our Christian obedience in the total ministry of the Church.

3. A re-examination of the whole scope and purpose of theological education. This is to be seen as preparation of the whole people of God for their ministry in the world. The training of the clergy cannot be considered apart from the training of the laity and both should be understood as one enterprise. This means:

(a) Clergy need to be trained in an understanding of the world in which the people will minister, and in an understanding of their own responsibility for pointing the people to that ministry and equipping them for it.

(b) Lay training needs to be understood in terms of preparing the people for the increasing complexity of their ministry in the world.

(c) Provision must be made for training both clergy and laity for specialized tasks.[72]

From the perspective of the need to go beyond provincial and national preoccupations in order to establish the supranational, regional and worldwide institutions necessary for the divine expression of the catholicity of the Church and of humanity, it is imperative that the Churches support the building of strong agencies of regional cooperation and concern themselves closely with political developments at the regional level.[73]

Thus, by the repentance that permits it to discern its insufficiencies and to provide a remedy for them, the Church is renewed and enabled to accept more fully the responsibilities entrusted to it by its Lord. In this permanent struggle against itself, against the forces of evil in political, economic and social garb that are at work within and around it, the Church can sustain the permanent process of renewal, continual repentance and correction, for it knows that these are the terms of her final triumph over the forces that undermine Church and humanity.

3. The Persevering and Triumphal Church

In spite of its unfaithfulness and treachery, which it is invited to correct every day by a continual reformation of its thought, behavior and institutions, the Church can voyage victoriously through all these failures, contradictions and sufferings because it knows that its success is assured — not by its virtues, but only by the grace of Christ whose body it is and whose triumph over all the forces of destruction was made manifest at Easter.

A deferred triumph   Of course, this victory, which has already been attained, has not yet become fully manifest and will not become so before the end of time. God's promise "Behold, I make all things new"[74] includes for us the hope that God will himself bring about salvation, justice and peace. "Behold, all is made new."[75] This word includes the certainty that in Christ the new reconciled creation has already dawned. The Church lives in this certainty and presses on toward this hope.[76]

A resolute advance   This pressing forward implies that we turn away from that which separates us from Christ, and slough off that which hinders our obedience to him. It changes also our political thinking and acting. We are directed away from anxiety, resignation, self-assertion and oppression by guilt, toward openness and solidarity with all men, toward the venture of trust and the readiness to sacrifice for constructive solutions. The aim of our political thinking and acting is to benefit and help men.

This is also the aim of many non-Christians, and leads us to cooperation with them in concrete tasks. In so doing our particular contribution will be made not only in the sober realization that all we do remains inadequate and limited, but also in our unshakable hope in him who says, "Behold, I make all things new."[77]

An immutable hope   This pressing forward in hope and

daily renewal is based on two certainties: the pardon that permits all renewal and the definitive triumph of Christ over all
the forces of destruction and death. These two certainties are
the basis of the most active of hopes.

Constantly renewed pardon by faith is the force that
liberates from all paralyzing guilt, from all sterile discouragement, and which permits and justifies all the renewals of history. Our hope is in him who made all things new. He judges our
structures of thought and action and renders them obsolete.[78]
We know the reality of sin and the depth of its hold on human
beings, and on our political and economic structures. But we
do not despair in spite of the resistance of men and structures,
with all their delays and frustrations, because we know that it
is God's world, and that in Christ there is forgiveness and the
chance to begin anew every day, step by step. God wants the
world to develop, and he conquers and will conquer sin.[79]
We act now, but our goal is limitless. Our time-horizon is long,
and this is why we go on hoping, as long as we act today and
do what we can.

We do not despair because of setbacks that seem serious,
so long as our actions today have their own target dates and
immediate objectives as part of a long-term process of development.[80] We are aware of the reality of sin and the depth of
its hold on men. Political and economic structures groan under
the weight of terrible injustice, but we do not lose hope, because we know that we are not a toy in the hands of blind
fate. In Christ God came into our world and our institutions
and has already gained the victory over all "principalities and
powers." His Kingdom comes, and with it his judgment and
mercy. The present state of affairs, which bodes ill for the
future, causes us great distress and anguish. But we cherish
this hope: that distress and selfishness among nations will
eventually be overcome by a stronger desire for mutual collaboration and a heightened sense of solidarity.[81]

The triumph is certain, though presently only glimpsed   This
final victory is now of course seen only from afar, by glimpses
here and there in history and in time, visible to the eyes of
faith. Nor can we know exactly what it will be, either for
Christ or for ourselves.[82] But we do know that it will be. The
Apostle Paul brought to our attention that the transfigured

Christ, the new Adam, is in fact the end and the beginning of all human history.[83] The race of Adam to which we yet belong is only a prefiguration of the new humanity, already inaugurated by Christ and his Kingdom in our time but whose full expansion will take place around the New Man, the resurrected Christ, the goal of history. One can even say that, with regard to John 1, Colossians 1 and Hebrews 1, the last Adam is the original one, meant and implied in the creation of the first. All this gives us the image of one great movement from lower to higher, going through estrangement and crisis, but also through atonement and salvation, and so directed toward its ultimate goal, a glorified humanity, in full communion with God, of which goal the risen Christ is the guarantee and the first-fruits.[84]

Ceaseless combat   It must not be forgotten, however, that this march of humanity toward freedom is a combat, a moment-by-moment struggle against adverse forces that sow discord, degradation, exploitation, oppression, hate and death. Though the final victory is promised, the individual phases of the battle enjoy no such promise. History is a battlefield where God squares off against the powers of sin and destruction.

Shared suffering   Though the victory of Easter is permanent, the defeat of Good Friday is daily renewed and neither the world nor the Church is spared its sufferings.[85] And even though God remains master of routed humanity throughout the murky battle and governs the nations by patience in order to guide history to its goal,[86] man's suffering, a reflection of Christ's passion, fills the individual's history as well as that of societies and nations with tragic meaning.[87] The groans, cries and birth-pangs of a creation longing for its fulfilment[88] have not ceased ringing out in this time when all the "former things" are said to pass away.[89] The Church lives out its active hope through, not alongside, this tragedy.[90] In the resurrection of Jesus a new creation was born, and the final goal of history was assured, when Christ as head of that new humanity will sum up all things.[91]

Persistence through tragedy   It is, then, in the tragic era of the anticipation of Christ's victory, already gained but not

fully manifest, that human history and that of the Church un-
fold, requiring of everyone combat and suffering, patience and
hope. We know that we never live the fulness of what we
profess, and we long for God to take over. Yet we rejoice that
already we can anticipate in worship the time when God will
renew us, all men, when he will "make all things new."[92]

We hear the cry of those who long for peace; of the hungry and exploited who demand bread and justice; of the
victims of discrimination who claim human dignity; and of
the increasing millions who seek for the meaning of life. God
also hears these cries and judges us. He speaks the liberating
Word.

The time for anticipatory action   We hear him say: I go
before you. Now that Christ carries away your sinful past, the
Spirit frees you to live for others. Anticipate my Kingdom in
joyful worship and daring acts. Trusting in God's renewing
power, let us join in these anticipations of God's Kingdom,
showing now something of the newness that Christ will complete.[93] We must travel this road together, united in mind and
heart. Hence we feel it necessary to remind everyone of the
seriousness of this issue in all its dimensions, and to impress
upon them the need for action. The moment for action has
reached a critical juncture. Can countless innocent children be
saved? Can countless destitute families obtain more humane
living conditions? Can world peace and human civilization be
preserved intact? Every individual and every nation must face
up to this issue, for it is their responsibility.[94]

In the final analysis, it is in this dark and uncertain advance, whose only certainty is the certainty of faith in the
final outcome and the sureties given by God, that the daily
task of every man and of every Christian is to be found. We
do not claim to have the answers, but rather we seek answers
in collaboration with all men. We try to see God's will in our
time and we would do this in collaboration with men of
other religions. We look for the next step that the facts before
us require of us. We can see a vision of the world in which
the so-called haves and have-nots work together to change each
other's structures so that the resources and talents of the world
are used to mutual advantage. We can see a vision of the
world in which men share their mutual gifts for the common

good of all. We dare to hope that this vision is more than a mirage.[95]

Only one criterion   And in this forward march the only criterion of truth and action that we possess to evaluate our short-term as well as our long-term behavior is the true figure of man, Christ the New Man. The only authentic figure of a valid society is the Kingdom he has inaugurated. Man has been renewed in Christ. It is by this truth that we must judge and repudiate the tragic distortions of humanity in the life of mankind, some found even in the Christian community.[96] Our goal is to discover in the world around us, on the basis of this criterion, enriched by all the knowledge gained from the Old and New Testaments, the manifold signs of the renewal wrought by the invisible Christ.

Many signs, but often ambiguous   Men are now inclined to react against all kinds of social, racial and economic discrimination and to strive with all their strength for world peace and global cooperation. In all this may be seen realizations of God's purposes for this world, signs of the coming Kingdom. We dare not use a stronger word than "signs," however, because the present universalizing of history partakes of that ambiguity which is characteristic of this world in its preliminary and sinful phase. With the signs of Christ's active presence, with the signs of his Kingdom in this world, are mixed the signs of the antichrist at work. Universal history, experienced apart from Christ, can become a threat as well as a blessing. The creation of a well-balanced, smoothly organized, technically perfect universal welfare-state is not the final goal of humanity. A society that has no purposes beyond its own welfare must die, and we can already see, in the abundant society whose only goal is abundance itself, the signs of a society dying of boredom. Will it not, out of sheer boredom, devote its superfluous powers to new irrational and even antihumane adventures? Progress in unification and technology is not *in itself* a good thing. The value of universal history depends on the good it serves and the goal toward which it is directed. The goal assigned to it by God is the only valid one. It must yet undergo much suffering, much devastation, many catastrophes, if it accepts intermediate goals as final.[97]

What a marvelous task and what an exalted responsibility are the Church's, whose mission is to remind men in all places and at all times of the goal fixed for human destiny and for all human action! That it might carry out this responsibility correctly, the Church must not be content with preaching a religion of inner spiritual life or of the eternal life to come. It must also testify to the love God has shown the whole world for the entire precious span of its history. It must, with Christ, bear the worry of man's temporal salvation, the sign of his eternal salvation.

Conclusion   In spite of the innumerable powers that would destroy and distort humanity, which are at work in history paralyzing the full, harmonious development of man, God is at work in the person of Christ, continually renewing the entire world in its economic, social and political life, and the Church community itself. In spite of its powerful attraction toward death and destruction, seemingly propelled in that direction by a force from within, humanity is led and continually renewed in its march toward the triumphant life won for it by Christ.

This march is stumbling and in darkness, but its outcome is certain. Christ's own victory over death and the various powers of destruction is the proof whose evidence bursts forth in faith. Easter will be the morning of the world until its end. And it is the role of Christians to discern in their temporal history the innumerable signs of this new dawn given to men by Christ.

Four: temporary tragedy and temporary politics

The world's march toward life, led by Christ who has already won victory over the destructive forces yet provisionally at work in the world, shows us the true dynamic condition of humanity, its true nature and its authentic goal. But before the full manifestation of this triumph, the world and the Church continue their march through darkness.

A. TEMPORARY TRAGEDY

The sounding points of this advance on the future, the points where the true condition of man and society are revealed, are Good Friday and Easter morning — a Good Friday whose manifestations are repeated daily in our time and in our history; and an Easter dawn whose reality is projected throughout this history, giving it dynamic meaning and a final goal.

The permanence of Easter and Good Friday   We have already discussed the meaning of the shadow stretching from Good Friday over all of human history. It is the failure of man's calling, his inability to understand and fulfil his true human condition, to make his authentic humanity a reality. It is the degradation of all human, cultural, social, economic and political relations. It is the failure of society, leading to the annihilation of civilizations and the self-inflicted death of humanity. But the failure is not fatal. Neither necessity nor fatality presides over the world's destiny. To the contrary. The victory of Easter attests that Christ, taking on once and for all the condemnation and death of humanity, is stronger than the destructive forces at work in creation.[1]

We have therefore attempted also to recognize the light of Easter in the renewal of all creation. We have tried to discern Christ's working in the continual, and occasionally revolutionary, transformation of the human condition and of societal structures. This transformation may be seen by the eyes of faith in the renewal of humanity manifested in the birth and daily rebirth of the Church. Pentecost also shows a certain continuity.

Good Friday: temporary   The proximity of Easter and Good Friday in our own time is very meaningful. It reveals the precarious position of every human purpose, of all society, of civilization itself. Death is a permanent threat and the tragedy of man's condition can appear at any moment, with its full gauntlet of horrors, suffering and sadness. Evil is active to the end of time and can from moment to moment manifest its grip on individuals and on social groups by suggesting to them the worst misdeeds. For a Christian, no atrocity in history is surprising, for, no matter how horrible it is, it is never more than an echo of what man was capable of doing when he denied and crucified the Son of God.

Easter: definitive   But the weight of this threat is not infinite. Evil has no definitive power over the world. Its empire is already surrounded, encircled and limited. It has been contained, mastered. The Easter victory proves that the final word on destiny has already been spoken by the God of love, that the end of human history and of every man is within his power. The time of tragedy is still our time, but it is limited and temporary.[2] The work of Pentecost is to make this victory certain to the eyes of faith and to make manifest its results. Thus, for a Christian, no feat, no human exploit, no genuine success is surprising, no matter how marvelous. For they are so many signs of the coming final triumph of humanity announced by the Easter victory, the most marvelous cause for surprise.

The time of temporary politics   The time of temporary tragedy will last as long as temporal history. In this time Christ combats for humanity and associates in this struggle men of all nations and all conditions. His purpose is to master the powers of individuals and society in order to organize them for growth, development and peace for individuals and for all mankind. It is, then, a time for the triumph of God's Kingdom, but the time that precedes it and announces its coming: the time of temporary politics. And because this time is also the time of temporary tragedy, the politics is also precarious. It is forever threatened, but always full of hope. It must forever be reactivated because it is forever modified by the advances of destructive evil and of triumphant life. It is the time in which we live, a time of extraordinary dynamics in men and in society, a vigor due to the power of the opposing forces in permanent combat. This dynamic power is active for life as well as for death, for the liberation, promotion and development of man as well as for his enslavement and oppression. The march of history is always uncertain and tragic, but it leads toward an end that is certain.

Society on the march   Church and society are together on this march toward the coming Kingdom, on this itinerary of human history.[3] They are both advancing toward a goal that only the Church knows by faith, whose approach it can discern by a few early signs.[4]

It is this basic condition of humanity, that of marching toward a goal both far off and daily attainable, which makes politics important, dignified, but also relative, precarious and inevitably chaotic.

The relative nature of every political project and choice
Since this is the situation, no political project whatever can be presented as absolute and sacred. No temporal society, present or future, can claim full identity with the Kingdom of God. The best it can hope for is to carry out some aspects of its role that will foreshadow the perfection of the Kingdom. But neither is any society completely bad.[5] Every society bears traces and signs attesting the nearness of God's Kingdom. And none may be flatly rejected as deprived of any promise or hope. It is therefore the duty of the Church, acquainted with the nature of the coming Kingdom and with its characteristics — even though its knowledge can never go beyond approximation — to perceive and announce the signs of this Kingdom. And it is also its duty to denounce any attempt at presenting a political project, whatever it may be, as absolute and sacred. Throughout its career, its duty is tirelessly to emphasize the necessary and useful nature of politics, alongside its temporal and relative character. It is important that this itinerant aspect of every society be constantly repeated,[6] for everything said and

done in politics, everything undertaken in the city to found or reform institutions, to organize territories and economic and social life (by recommending certain choices or certain courses of action over others), is always based on a very precarious and uncertain appreciation of reality. The only ethical worth in a given temporal undertaking lies in its hidden relationship to the Kingdom of God, and this relationship is always difficult to establish. Every human project is thus vitiated by relativity and precariousness: its only value is transitory. And nothing undertaken by man can be declared fully in conformity to the will of Jesus Christ. Nothing in this march, where even Christians can see Christ only as in a glass darkly, can be more than a reflection of his will, than a glimpse of the Kingdom, than a movement, a sign, necessary, indispensable for the growth and development of society and of the city, but always temporary, always to be reconsidered, always to be re-evaluated by the measure of Christ and his Kingdom. And this judgment itself must constantly be revised in terms of changing circumstances and according to the new historical and scientific data of each situation.

The eternal nature of every political project and choice
This does not mean that political choice, though relative, is not a very important choice: good or bad, it directs men's lives. For the Christian, as we have seen, the political act is one of the practical works by which his true faith is visibly expressed before men and before God. It is as important as any other decision. The practice of politics is no less worthy than the practice of religion. For, as we have said, man's calling in Christ implies a response involving his entire being and existence, material and physical as well as religious, temporal as well as spiritual.

Now, all ethical works and decisions are weakened by a degree of uncertainty that forbids Christians from ever predicting which works will be accepted by God as works worthy of faith.[7] There is always, therefore, *an unavoidable risk in action,* a risk inherent in the very nature of the commitment of Christian faith. Obedience always includes for the Christian a risk, but a risk taken in full confidence of God's love and pardon. In spite of this relativity, of this precariousness of human action, political projects do take on a sacred character in man's heart. For conscious Christians alone can know, because of their faith in Christ, the hidden goal of history. Others are inclined to sacralize politics and make it a substitute for faith. And Christians of declining faith are not exempt from this perversion. When danger threatens, a given national policy or ideology soon takes on a sacred character. And history teaches us that this sacredness is equally well linked with religion or with a secular or atheistic conception of life. Politics and ideologies easily take the place of God in man's heart.

The time of ideologies and utopias   The ideologies people provide for themselves to fill the emptiness of a final goal, to cover the uncertainty of their destiny, to justify their political or economic action or to feed their hopes are thus ideologies meant to replace faith or to be its substitute. To a great extent they deceive men, for they give him a reduced image of his destiny, a false idea of his own nature and an imaginary goal for society. They invent a portrait of ideal man and of tomorrow's society by giving an appearance of reality to the momentary dreams of a given social or national group, the products of alienation, of more or less conscious resentments and of idealized aspirations. Moreover, they furnish the members of the group with necessary heroes to worship and dream-destroying enemies to hate. They therefore set social groups, races and nations against each other, and provide for their aspirations and antagonisms a false justification. They exalt hate and vengeance by proposing sacred crusades. Finally, they engender illusion, deception, suffering and death.

The desecration of ideologies   It is therefore the Church's duty tirelessly to set these ideologies and utopias, all more or less illusory, over against the knowledge of Christ, the final and genuine goal of all of society and the one who can justify humanity's entire future.

In all these historical ideologies, however, each a more or less secular form of religion, as in every non-Christian religion, in every human aspiration, in every political ideal, in every dream and in every utopia (the idols of men and societies), there are elements of truth, there are traces of the groanings of creation for its deliverance, there is an echo of the work

of renewal, restoration and development Christ has undertaken in leading the world toward its end.

The need to save a part of ideology   One of the Church's
functions, then, while ever proclaiming anew the concrete
social and political message of the Gospel and the ethics of
the Kingdom of God, is to criticize ideologies that fuel the
hopes of whole populations and stimulate their conservative
or revolutionary ardor. Such criticism is indispensable, for, in
every one of the values men consider to be definitive when in
fact they are only temporary, there may be glimpsed through
the fog of deceitfulness a glimmer of the coming Kingdom,
there may be discovered or rediscovered something of the Kingdom Christ inaugurated in history, toward which all peoples
are marching.

The Gospel, let us repeat, is a critical Gospel, proclaiming the judgment of God and his grace toward all human
values, activities and dreams. For in Christ the New Man, and
his Kingdom, are found the beginning, the touchstone and the
end of all human destiny.[8] The Church must therefore dissoci-
ate the ideological husk—which, as such, is to be thrown away—
from the valuable kernel. It must pass in review the concrete
historical goals, short-term and long-term, that the ideology
supposes. It must examine the practical means proposed to
carry out each of the goals and estimate the value of the goals
and the means, by comparison with the norms of Christ and
his Kingdom and according to the present historical conditions
rightly assessed.

When, for example, liberal ideology sounds the rallying-
cry for a titanic struggle in favor of individual liberty, the
Church must make clear what is historically correct and incorrect in this ambiguous struggle. By fighting against the collectively oppressive constraints of the old regime and destroying
them, the liberal factions of the eighteenth and nineteenth
centuries constituted a liberating ideology. By stimulating
individual human initiative and responsibility against the alienating power of the group, this ideology created irreplaceable
values that maintain all of their dignity. But by stimulating
and justifying the triumph of the strong over the weak and by
ignoring the violent and oppressive character that the domination of the rich over the weak and poor can assume even with-

in a perfectly legal frame of action, it breaks the bond of human solidarity and becomes one of humanity's most destructive forces.

And when, in reaction to the collective tyranny of the rich and powerful, socialism proclaims the need for solidarity felt by the oppressed and tries to organize its human and social realization, this ideology exhibits its positive and creative nature. But when it in turn sets up structures that hamper the development of other essential human values, when it thus brings about new forms of tyranny by minorities and tends to destroy the unique and peculiar character of every individual in creation by requiring complete conformity to the social group, by that very constraint it becomes a dangerous ideology to be resisted. In short, the Christian must be aware of the particular conditions, past and present, in which the various ideologies are struggling, and must be able to discern the essential human values each of them is attempting to safeguard. His task, then, is to save these values by joining in the limited struggle that can foster their preservation. His action will thus be gauged by *an order of priority that will vary according to historical conditions.*

The need to create realistic utopias   The Church must not be content to work with foreign material. Its role has not been fulfilled when it has criticized secular ideologies. Since it has its own model for society (Christ and his Kingdom), which is already beginning to form in the world, it must propose to every society, in its time and place, *relative models* that can incorporate concrete goals capable of bringing about or developing human values whose promotion and growth constitute a sign of the coming Kingdom.

When, for example, man's real human liberties are threatened, the Church must not hesitate to recommend — as a temporary but necessary goal — a model of secular liberty. Or when a minimum standard of economic or social justice is contradicted by concrete facts, the Church must propose, and join with others who propose, a model of a just society, even if this relative goal cannot be attained completely or immediately. For the great project of the coming Kingdom must produce, for the reality of temporal existence, smaller projects whose duration is not guaranteed but which can show analogies to the great Kingdom while being feasible in a reasonable amount of time. Thus the Church's duty, for example, is perpetually to present to the world the goals of peace, non-violence, liberty, solidarity, disarmament, classless society, global society, etc., and to work for their political realization, even if the goals may not be immediately reached — for these political attempts are directed *toward* the coming Kingdom.

On the other hand, Christians must denounce as unrealistic those political projects which are in obvious contradiction to the coming of the Kingdom. The Church's vision enables it to distinguish between *realistic utopias,* projects that anticipate the Kingdom but are nonetheless essentially in agreement with its nature, and *fanciful utopias.* The latter, though occasionally based on popular feeling capable of promising early realization, are from the beginning doomed to failure because they are contrary to the figure of the New Man and of the society to be (like Hitler's dream of Aryan hegemony, for example, or the unequal development of races in one society).

Political realism   Because only the Church in its faith in the Master of history can know the destiny of any policy, and because, on the other hand, it lives in a world where a distorted humanity ascribes to its political goals incorrect values and impossible hopes, its position is ambiguous. It cannot accept the ideologies as they stand. It must carry out its secularizing function toward them. But it must at the same time collaborate with those who are partisan to these ideologies, for the work of building a city is a common work that could never be limited exclusively to Christians. Without following the ideology of the movement, then, the Church must collaborate for the success of the relative concrete goals contained in the given ideologies, to the extent that these are in even distant accord with the requirements of the Kingdom of God. The fact that a given ideology is not in conformity to its faith does not release the Church from participating in the struggles that will assure the attainment of whatever truth is contained in the ideology. Christian politics is from this perspective, therefore, a *politics of compromise;* for, though they do not share the ideological illusion of unbelievers or of religious persons captivated by ideology, Christians must go with them to the end of the road and must join in their enterprises for the success of valid temporal goals. On the other hand, it would be completely wrong for the Church to attempt to force unbelievers into accepting a given policy because it is relatively closer to the criteria of the Kingdom of God. In their necessary collaboration with the nonbelievers who with them make up the civil community, Christians may propose only policies based on concrete secular goals. Though they can discern the analogous or dialectical relationships of these goals with the work of Christ, the final destiny of these goals cannot be recognized without faith. The Church must, therefore, avoid a clerical policy of forcing the civil community to accept goals that exist by faith. Only concrete secular objectives — political objectives — that conform to the Church's distant spiritual or theological goals may be validly proposed to non-Christians. In other words, temporal goals must be gauged by criteria of the Kingdom, but they must always be translated into terms of *political, secular goals,* and must be understood as *temporary goals.* Returning to the two dominant ideologies mentioned above, political and economic liberalism on the one hand and collectivism on the other, the fact that the first is more or less tolerant of religion (as long as it is not condemned by the Church), while the second is usually associated with atheism, must not be the determining factor in the Christian's political assessment. For both of these ideologies contain human truths some of which are in agreement with what the Gospel reveals as true human nature while others are opposed. Placed in their historical context, there are places and times where each of them puts top priority on partial truths concerning man and society that Christians themselves have forgotten and which should be considered anew in their own right. No Christian, then, may refuse to collaborate with partisans of these ideologies on the pretext that they are completely contrary to Christian faith. Rather it is this collaboration of thinking Christians, reserved yet active, which makes their political involvement the critical and useful factor in society that their faith invites them to furnish. And it is by such collaboration, without a taint of fanaticism and occasionally spiced with humor, that Christians may express today's ideologies, may secularize them and relativize them according to their calling in this time of temporary politics.

The political realism of thinking Christians is, therefore,

made up of accommodations fitted to the historical possibilities of a given time and place. It enables them to join with others who do not share their faith in fighting for just, but limited goals. It is a kind of historical opportunism based on ethical criteria. But it must not be confused with the sordid brand of realism and opportunism that is out only to capture, by any means, the interests of a nation, a social group, an individual or an ideology.

The political ethics of Christians   In this time when humanity is marching under the banner of temporary tragedy the Church's responsibility is tremendous. It is up to the Church to proclaim to the entire world, in its spiritual, cultural, social, economic and political activities, in all times and in all places, the final destiny of its labor and thus to give it a meaning that it is unable to find in itself. This responsibility is basic to the existence of the human race. For the world, despite the love and constant renewal communicated to it by Christ, does not know where it is going; man does not know who he is and societies cannot know the essential reason for their existence. If, therefore, the Church does not proclaim to the whole world, to all peoples and to all societies, their final destiny and the meaning of daily existence, men, without guidance, make their activities and fancies into final goals.

The essential difference between the Church and the world lies in the fact that the world is unconsciously aspiring to liberation and final restoration,[9] while the Church knows and discerns by faith, as in a glass darkly,[10] for the Church has received the promised Spirit and thereby the gift of discernment.

Because it has received a glimpse of the end, it can dimly recognize in the world the signs that already manifest its anticipated realization.[11] On this discernment rest its ethical function and its mission as a sentinel or conscience for society. Because the Church's responsibility is constantly to remind the world and its political, economic and social institutions of *the end* assigned to them by God, it must also decide to what extent *the means* used are compatible with the end. And it must proclaim where *concrete projects* are announcing and *partially* realizing this destiny. We ought to develop here the method required by the Church's ethical function in and for the world — for such an ethics goes far beyond the social ethics of the individual to which Christian ethics have often been reduced. Let us point out only that the instrument of this ethics is all of biblical revelation, Old and New Testaments. For this revelation is the means whereby the knowledge of the New Man who inaugurates a new Kingdom is attained. And the coming of this Kingdom, already a part of temporal history although it is not fully realized, presents for our contemplation today the *first-fruits* of the future transformation to which the whole earth is called. The Church must, therefore, engage in a rigorous analysis, done as scientifically as possible, of the historical, economic, social and political conditions by which it is surrounded, so as to be able to compare these data with biblical data and recognize the signs of social renewal that attest that the Kingdom it is proclaiming is actually present.[12-13]

The double aspect of the Church's political function, requiring a double method of analysis to formulate its ethics, has been correctly defined as "scrutinizing the signs of the times and interpreting them in the light of the Gospel."[14]

The necessity for the Church to examine its politics   In order to understand correctly the grandiose yet humble mission of the Church, and its means of action, we must remember to what extent it is itself subject to the historical condition of humanity, that is, to what extent it, the Church, and perhaps first of all the Church, is the place where the unequal duality of Good Friday and Easter is manifested in combat. (It is proper to speak of unequal duality because the weight of Good Friday, though it oppresses mankind until its death and condemnation, is, as it were, finally thrust aside by the triumph of Easter and the many signs already present of the soon-coming liberation of all of creation.[15]) Caught up in this titanic battle, the Church is itself tossed about between the opposing forces and becomes occasionally an accomplice of the forces oppressing men, without being aware of it. If, then, it is to fulfil correctly its critical role, it must determine to what extent its behavior is governed by its socio-political environment; to what extent this environmental conditioning is compatible with its mission; and to what extent it may legitimately accept to be taught and renewed by the changes and transformation taking place in the world and which contain some aspects of Christ's work of renewal.[16] This implies that it must be humble enough and submissive enough to allow itself to be criticized by the eternally critical Gospel, bearer of eternal judgment and eternal pardon, and by a world in constant mutation, and to accept what is positive in the world's criticism.

Where and how the Church may become politically involved
The Church's role, as we have seen, is to proclaim the good news of the renewal of all things by Jesus Christ, and it is thus the bearer of a most essential message for all human politics, educational, cultural, social, economic and civic. Its first responsibility, as we have just pointed out, is to discern the signs of the times,[17] that is, to scrutinize every place and every moment in history to determine where Christ is at work. Now the Gospel tells us that he is with all who suffer, who are oppressed, whose dignity is scorned, whose basic rights are threatened. The Church must, therefore, follow its Master's example, speaking and acting where human lives or human dignity is endangered, and where opportunities for a better future are neglected.[18] Here is where its attention and action must have top priority. But if it wants to go beyond the role of bandage-binder for humanity, if it decides to act against the causes of oppression and injustice and positively to follow its master in establishing a new Kingdom, to invite men and societies to the constructive tasks of unity, development and peace, it must accept an *avant-garde* role in planning and carrying out action in all areas.

An arbitrary distinction: temporal and spiritual   Here the important question must be asked: Who is the Church and who does what? The old and too often traditional answer that ecclesiastical institutions and the ministry alone are to preach while the laity are to draw the practical and political conclusions of this teaching is too simplistic. Moreover, it is false. For though it is true that Christ never formulated a political program, his preaching, witnessing and proclamation of the Kingdom by his acts so radically called in question the social and political conceptions and behavior of his time that he was objectively, judicially condemned as a subversive politico-religious agitator.[19] A pastoral sermon that touches only the Christian's inner spiritual life (or, in evangelization, that of the future believer) and his salvation for the life to come, without touching the temporal salvation of man and society within a definite historical framework, is not a sermon in accord with the good news of the present liberating arrival of the new Kingdom. An ecclesiastical institution that takes no risks for the temporal liberation of the poor and oppressed is not bearing testimony to the living incarnation of the God of love. We have already seen how much all aspects of society, economic, political and social, need to know the source of renewing power and its concrete purpose in order to be able to avoid seeing their forces rapidly turn into forces of oppression and degradation. Have the social sciences not taught us how closely related and interwoven are the political, economic, social and spiritual activities of a given society? It is not, therefore, according to an artificial, unevangelical and unrealistic separation between the spiritual and the temporal, one reserved for the ministry and the other for the laity, that the Church's mission is to be understood. Of course the distinction between the temporal and the spiritual is essential, permitting the proper differentiation between what comes from God and what pertains to man. But it must never be used to divide the human being into one part that is autonomous and not under Christ's direction (such as politics, for example), and another part that would be for Christ (such as the religious life, for example).

A proper pastoral discernment   Rather, the Church's mission must be examined with a proper assessment of the necessities of a given time and place, in an intimate and preserving collaboration between clergy and laity. Of course any policy considered by the clergy with the intent of establishing the domination of society by Christians or ecclesiastical institutions must be condemned and banished because it goes contrary to the very purposes of the Church itself. Founded to restore the Kingdom of Heaven here on earth and not to conquer earthly territory, the Church affirms clearly that the domains of the Church and the state are separate and that the two powers, ecclesiastical and civil, are each sovereign in its sphere.[20] But as the possessor of humanity, it cannot help — indeed it is its duty — but proclaim the multiple consequences of this vision through all areas of life. It cannot, therefore, keep from warning and encouraging, from trying in every situation of life to discern the positive action that appears most clearly in conformity to the requirements and promises of Christ.

Honest, unprejudiced dialog   And since every secular policy brings a doctrine into play, a certain conception of life, there is no way the Church can avoid coming into frequent contradiction with certain aspects of these doctrines. It cannot, however, issue a blanket condemnation of them. For, as we have said, the Church must be careful not to identify itself fully with a given political institution, but its duty calls it to enter into dialog with all who would build the city. And since it is a city open to all, the dialog must be open to all, without exception, with no distinctions of a religious or ideological nature. Such a dialog is necessary first of all to help the Church not to become identified (in spite of its legitimate preferences in this era of the temporary) with a particular political program, and secondly to enable the Church to recognize and declare what is constructive and legitimate, by Christ's standards, in each different program. For as Christians we believe that Christ speaks in honest dialog, that he reveals himself to those who do not know him and that he corrects our limited, distorted understanding of the Gospel.[21] The result of such a dialog is that Christians are free to fight along with others, with no ideological or partisan program, to attain the particular, limited political goals that correspond to a given concrete problem.[22] Church unity (local and worldwide) is a lie if it is established *without consideration* for divergent political and ethical choices. It can be authentic only if it dominates, and relativizes, the necessary choices and the antagonisms that will be their inevitable result. In order to attain such unity the Churches must accustom Christians to take responsibility for the political tensions *within* their communion by favoring confrontations and dialog voluntarily undertaken and followed.

The ambiguity of all Christian witnessing   In this political witnessing Christians must realize that, just as the words by which they testify of Christ appear to unbelievers to be human or religious words with no more credibility than the words of any other person or religion, their political testimony, without the eyes of faith, will not appear to be an explicit rendering of their obedience to Jesus Christ. They are easily confused with the acts and words of anyone else acting on any motivation. Only the Holy Spirit can give to words and acts the ability to convey the Christian witness, the Christian revelation. Only the Holy Spirit can inspire and thus authenticate a social or political act and give it the value of a spiritual communication.[23] Christians can, therefore, as for any personal, individual act, maintain a constant search for faithful social conduct consonant with how they understand Christ and his Kingdom and thus will be able to carry out political acts in analogical agreement with their faith. It is on this condition that their acts will carry an authentic testimony in spite of their precariousness, in spite of their ambiguous and temporary nature.

In our time the Churches have recognized that such politics, though temporary and contingent, must be conducted in terms of a certain number of priorities.

B. A SOLIDARY CITY AND A GLOBAL HOMELAND

The first and most important task is to make everyone understand that the new world in which we live promises exceptional possibilities to mankind, augmenting his responsibility to master them and to put them in God's plan manifested in Christ for the unity, solidarity and development of humanity. The vast problem of how to control modern technological society and subject it to human, temporal goals, consciously decided and democratically adopted, is thus laid upon the Christian conscience. We are not going to deal here with the details of this tremendous goal, however important that may be for the future of industrial society and all civilization. The limits of this work do not permit it. The following lines, then, are intended only to trace a general perspective of the urgent action that the present generation must undertake. The ecumenical texts being studied here provide more ample treatment of practical details. But their counsels must be constantly revised as local, regional and global circumstances evolve.[24]

The primary necessity: a general realization of (a) *the new possibilities, and* (b) *the gross inequalities*   We live in a new world of exciting prospects. For the first time in history we know that all men could enjoy the prosperity that has hitherto been enjoyed by a few. The adventure of cooperation with all men for the development of the earth for all men is open for all of us. As today we have the means, so we are without the excuse of ignorance about the condition of men throughout the earth. It is one world, and the gross inequalities between the peoples of different nations and different continents are as inexcusable as the gross inequalities within nations.[25]

Create a common will to change   To attain this, the first step is to create an opinion favorable to voluntary, positive participation in the changes of economic and political structure necessitated by the realization of the common development of social groups and nations. For where the powers of individual, social and national special interests are opposed to change, development appears impossible.[26] Change may be effected only by establishing new structures capable of democratically controlling economic growth and subjecting it to common human goals consciously chosen.

Create a will for better collaboration   To reach this goal it is necessary to envisage and bring about an increasing collaboration between all the members of society and of the Churches. And though we may emphasize different aspects of doctrine, we know that God is at work in the development taking place today, that he is calling us to work with him, to work in common with each other and with all men who are engaged in this work, whatever their beliefs.[27]

A better division of the fruits of development   To ensure common development it is not enough to ensure economic growth. It is also necessary for the growth to be controlled and subjected to goals arranged according to explicit priorities democratically fixed. Thus, by an equitable division of revenue for the common good, it can be of profit to all. From the Christian point of view, we have seen, the implicit goal of development is to free man and enable him to make intelligent use of the creative power given to him by God. Every worker must participate consciously in the goals of collective effort, and these goals must be established democratically. The distribution of income must be more equitable. Social integration must eliminate class barriers.[28] Such solidarity must be visible within a given nation as well as among nations. There must be a struggle against poverty on the local as well as the international level without radically separating local and international issues. The rich countries cannot use poverty at home as an excuse for doing nothing abroad. But the local emphasis will be different in the realization of universal solidarity. The developing countries will stress their local problems and obligations of social change, and the rich countries will emphasize their commitment to world justice.[29]

Developing countries   In underdeveloped regions the strategy must deal with:

Growth Rate. The developing countries must achieve a much more rapid rate of growth. Each country must exert intensified effort while demanding more effective international development effort. The basic responsibility for development will continue to lie with the developing countries themselves. The diversity of these countries in resources, culture and political structure means that no single strategy can serve their needs to modernize. Even so, certain economic and social problems of great urgency are common to most of them.

Social Justice. This is a goal of first priority to ensure harmonious human development over the whole world and an increasingly active participation by everyone in economic development.

Agriculture. Since agriculture is the largest economic activity in all developing countries, its problems are central to progress. Moreover, improving social conditions in the rural sector also deserves high priority. Often there is an almost complete lack of education, health facilities, electrification and other requirements of human living. Society generally remains stratified and is often too stagnant. Leaders must mobilize and inspire their people and work against the traditions, structures and political forces standing in the way of economic and social progress. In this effort, religious groups have an important part to play in instilling the new values needed, based on receptiveness to change and creativity, to work and achievement, to social consciousness and cooperation, and to planning and saving for the future. The creation of a feeling of national solidarity can facilitate political stability by going beyond certain ethnic problems and thus free energy for development.

The struggle to improve agriculture must be maintained because backward agriculture affects the whole economy by keeping income down and limiting purchasing power for other services and products. It provides inadequate supplies of raw materials for industry and for income-earning exports. Necessary food imports divert foreign exchange from the purchase of capital goods. Production, distribution and use of farm products must all be improved. The use of fertilizers, the development of irrigation, the production of new seed strains are all indispensable improvements.

The Industrial Sector. Industry must be developed with the purpose of supplying the internal market while serving an integral role in the regional and international economy. It includes, therefore, the establishment of an internal and international *commercial network,* integrated into a balanced international economic system.

The Demographic Factor. This is often the determining factor in regional growth and must of course be considered in the context of local conditions.

Education. Education must be related to manpower needs and must therefore be an essential part of development strategy.

Role of Governments. This is a decisive and central role. The preparation of a national development plan, to the extent that it is carried out, is the only way to make a wise use of human and financial resources. The creation of common markets should enable regional economic groups to form, and this in turn will create larger markets and bring together larger pools of funds for investment. The overall needs of the region would thus be met, and at the same time a basis for competition on the world market would be provided.

The developed countries   Within the developed countries the strategy must deal first of all with a *radical qualitative improvement* of their commercial, economic, financial and political relations with the weaker countries. The next level of concern should be with the *volume and quality of help.* These countries must dedicate a larger part of their budgetary resources to international cooperation and must reverse present priorities that favor the defense and space budgets. They must increase the transfer of capital toward the developing countries without unreasonably increasing the international debt of the countries enjoying the use of these capital investments. It is therefore necessary to revise both the *commercial conditions* and the *economic and financial conditions* in the relationships between rich and poor countries so that the oppressive effects of domination by the strong countries over the weak may be eliminated.

To carry this out, *international agencies* endowed with the necessary powers to attain these results must be strengthened and increased.[30] World development can be assured only by strengthening these structures and establishing worldwide plans whose principal points are chosen by all peoples rich and poor. The extraordinary means assembled by science and technology for the conquest of the moon prove that the mastery of gigantic collective problems is henceforth possible.

Revolution   The importance and urgency of all these modifications can bring about revolutionary situations in countries unwilling to face them. It is the role of leaders in the developing countries, as we have said, to mobilize and inspire their people to take up the responsibility of their own development. To bring this about they must work against the traditions, structures and political forces standing in the way of economic and social progress. To do so will require the use of all avenues of communication and influence. But if they are themselves the barrier to understanding and assuming the diversified responsibility for development, social groups must exert pressure to bring them to make the proper decision.[31] Where the maintenance of order is an obstacle to *just* order, some will decide for revolutionary action against that injustice, struggling for a just society without which the new humanity cannot fully come.[32]

Violence and nonviolence   But in such situations, what means are to be used? Whatever the case may be, when a revolutionary situation develops every effort must be made to achieve a nonviolent revolution. All our efforts must be directed to change without violence. But are there not extreme cases where the violence of the established order is so endemic that it necessitates a counter-violence to destroy it as soon as possible?

If injustice is so embedded in the status quo and its supporters refuse to admit change, then as a last resort men's conscience may lead them in full and clear-sighted responsibility, without hate or rancor, to engage in violent revolution. A heavy burden then rests on those who have resisted change.[33] We must, however, recognize that such violent changes are morally ambiguous. They can bring more woe than they eradicate. This is because violent revolution in itself does not solve a single problem. It can occasionally be an indispensable first step toward the harmonious development of society, but to be successful society does not need revolution but political stability, means of production, credit, a permanent educational system, rural progress, technology, tools, fertilizer, etc. That is why it is so important to develop — and this is one of the Church's most pressing tasks — workable strategies of nonviolent revolution and social transformation.[34] In any case, the problems of a just revolution are as involved as the problems of a just war, and the Church must maintain the rights of those who conscientiously believe they must participate in armed conflict, either in regular military service or in revolutionary warfare, as well as the rights of those who just as conscientiously believe they must oppose such participation.[35] Members of the same Church, though divided in their commitments for reasons clearly understood and based on faith, must continue meeting in order to assure a confrontation of their goals and motivations.

Further, it must be emphasized that top priority today must be given to integrating all political, economic and social action into a wider politics whose goal is to bring about an integrated and pluralistic society of worldwide dimensions.

A united worldwide society   The Churches are today emphatically emphasizing that we have now, for better or worse, entered the new era of a worldwide society that, in spite of its respect for the plurality of national particularities, is one and solidary.

This emphasis is surprising because the Churches' teaching has often been strongly affected by secular nationalistic doctrines, then disguised with religiosity and even confused with Christianity itself. This has influenced them to entrust their members with the development of the national community as their first political duty. Only secondarily, and rarely at that, have they taught that it was a duty to become interested in other nations and to struggle for international peace and justice.

Beyond the national state   The Churches' attitude has changed. Without minimizing the importance of the Christian's duties within his own nation, to the extent, for example, of preaching the need for young nations to develop their national consciousness and to put national interests over local or tribal considerations, they now teach that one of the Christian's first duties is to take his place in the struggle for the formation of a coherent and organic world society, endowed with the institutions necessary for its development.

The basic motivation for these frequently powerful calls to action is not pure historical opportunism, as one might first think. Rather, Christians are realizing that historical conditions are finally gelling to enable humanity to reach the fulness of its universal destiny.

And this universal destiny is not imagined as some fantastic utopia. It is rather the basic destiny of all nations, revealed to us, as we have seen, by the nature and calling of the Church, by its essence as a catholic and ecumenical institution.

This change of perspective is extremely important. It is based on the theological reflection we have studied that emphasizes the universal work accomplished by Christ in the world for the unity and harmonious development of humanity.

As long as Christian ethical teaching bases the duties of temporal existence only on the doctrine of creation, it is difficult to imagine how the Christian's duties could go beyond the national community. For the doctrine of order in creation easily postulates a world divided into nations as an unavoidable fact of nature. And, in this context, Christ's reconciling work touches only man's inner spiritual destiny and its realization in the world to come. The social teaching of today's Churches does not deny the work of creation, but nonetheless it rests on the rediscovery of an important aspect of the Gospel according to which Christ's act of redemption and reconciliation has an immediate effect on the destiny of all men and all nations, even if they are not aware of it. Christ's work illuminates, realizes and transfigures the order of creation, an order that alienated humanity cannot understand without benefit of revelation.

By rediscovering, therefore, the cosmic import of Christ's work and its interweaving into the fabric of the secular history of all peoples, the Churches have acknowledged the importance and urgency of their political, economic and social mission, that of fully restoring to social activities their meaning and final destiny. They perceive at the same time how relative and secondary racial and national relationships are when compared to the fundamental worldwide unity of humanity.[36]

Regional unity   The creation of a well-regulated world society must necessarily pass through the stage of regional unity. Today the national unit has become too small, particularly among the weaker nations. Both the need for self-protection against economic domination by more powerful nations and the mutual assistance in development afforded by economic cooperation suggest the desirability of regional organizations. These can contribute to peace both internally as an instrument of reconciliation between their members, and externally as a form of cooperative security. They offer a practical intermediate step toward the goal of one world community.[37]

World integration   It must not be forgotten, of course, that the political and social order we must continually create and re-create is a relative order. It is obvious that the establishment of regional units can create new sources of conflict and new imperialistic schemes even more powerful than the national forms of imperialism attested in history. That is why the creation of regional units must be integrated into the world structure of society. Their activities and objectives must be in accord with the United Nations Charter. Regional integration increases the risk of a division between rich and poor nations. These organizations therefore must conceive their role as one within the larger world community.[38]

The Churches must show the example by bursting their national and confessional structures   All the essential theological reasons we have mentioned indicate the primary role the Church can and must play in the critical elaboration of this multi-national order. This it can attain only by constant reference to the standards of Christ and his Kingdom, which are also those of the Church, and by translating these into temporal political terms. It is imperative that the Churches support the building of strong agencies of regional cooperation and concern themselves closely with political developments at the regional level. They must constantly maintain close cooperation,[39] and show the example by bursting their national and confessional structures. Confessionalism can represent the ecclesiastical equivalent of provincialism.

A new education   In order to realize this pluralistic world society, the purpose of which is to express, in this provisional time in history, an approximate figure of God's Kingdom and its organic catholicity, an educational initiative must be undertaken, dealing with the common development of the nations and the creation of citizens dedicated to developing the emergent world community. The development of a true sense of world citizenship requires first of all the recognition of the legitimate existence of a pluralistic international society.[40]

From destructive national armies to a common world development   In all countries the arms race is a latent source of international conflict as well as an unacceptable waste, both for the internal life of a nation and on the international level. When so many millions are starving, so many families are destitute, so many men are steeped in ignorance, so many people need schools, hospitals and homes worthy of the name, we cannot tolerate public and private expenditures of a wasteful nature, we cannot but condemn lavish displays of wealth by nations or individuals. We cannot approve a debilitating arms race. It is our solemn duty to speak out against them.[41]

This is why it is so important that all governments, separately and jointly, re-examine their priorities and give development and cooperation the central attention and prestige traditionally allotted to defense.[42] In order to facilitate the revision of priorities that must be effected both in individual mentalities and in governments, a portion of military expenditures must be set aside for a world development fund.[43] There should also be an interdiction of the international scandal inherent in the competitive exportation of arms, aggravating the dangers in many explosive situations. The discipline of a step-by-step disarmament must be accepted, in all categories of armaments.[44] Governments must recognize and sustain the different types of civil services oriented toward technical co-operation, and accord to them a rank at least equal with national service.[45] Such a conversion could be attained pro-gressively by the establishment of a national, then international development tax.[46] The establishment of an international political order requires important modifications in internation-al law.

The necessary development of international law   The for-mation of an international law code to ensure worldwide order and justice has not only a conserving and stabilizing function but also a dynamic and constructive role. To make this possible we must see the development of an international ethos, and the Churches have a big part to play in this.[47]

A world government   A worldwide authority must be estab-lished, capable of working effectively in the judicial and politi-cal arenas, enabling the agencies of the United Nations to unite in true cooperation not only a few powerful nations, but all peoples.[48] For Christians the indications contained in Paul's Epistle to the Romans (ch. 13) are legitimately applicable to a worldwide, supranational political structure. Responsible obedience to the teaching of the Scriptures requires their re-interpretation in terms of new historical situations.

The decisive international role of the Churches   For the one who understands the role in universal renewal that the Church of Jesus Christ is intended to play throughout the world, all these goals appear urgent and the church's participation in their realization appears to be one of the top priority tasks of our time. The Christian vision is one of profound interdepen-dence, of shared experience and support, of mankind working jointly at its own development and achieving together "the glorious liberty of the sons of God."[49] For this purpose, all the activities of the Churches must be put into the proper context of planetary interdependence and brotherhood.[50] It is thus imperative for Christians to acknowledge the profound spiritual motivation of this orientation of all their activities according to priorities. They must effect a global re-organization of all their Church structures.

The necessary mobilization of every parish   It is certain that an authentic Christian witness concerning the renewal of individual lives and social relationships, in all areas of cultural, economic and political life, must be expressed at the *parish level*. There is no parish so small or isolated that it should feel free of involvement in this common responsibility through prayer, education and consultation with Christians of the nations concerned and through ecumenical service and action at the local level.[51]

In order to facilitate a new understanding of their task, local parishes as well as regional and national Churches must become acquainted with modern ecumenical documents drawn up at the most important assemblies of our time (Vatican II, Beirut, Uppsala, etc.), and study their consequences for the Churches in question. Each Church should determine and apply the concrete implications of these recommendations based on an analysis of its local, regional and national situation.[52]

It is especially urgent that the Churches, in each parish, express in their own life the truth that all men are created equal in God's sight, and share a common humanity. In particular, they must move beyond the piecemeal and paternalistic programs of charity that have sometimes characterized Christian missions and must confront positively the systematic injustice of the world economy.

It is imperative that they strive actively and urgently for that reform of will and conscience among the people of the world which alone can inspire the achievement of greater international justice. To this end, the Churches should particularly concern themselves with political parties, trade unions and other groups influencing public opinion. Finally, they must give greater priority and more money to ministries of reconciliation and service on an international scale, especially where the most explosive forms of injustice are to be found.[53]

Once more: the Churches must be equipped   Most Churches are not organized and prepared to fulfil this essential mission, that of "equipping the saints for their ministry in the world,"[54] of being "the protesting conscience of society."[55] The problem, then, is not for them to know whether they are going to add new structures to the old but to ask themselves: "Are we totally structured for mission?"[56]

conclusion

An active hope   Christ's work in the world, appearing in full light on the cross of Golgotha on Good Friday, and in the first Christians on Easter and the following days, gives us an exact, realistic understanding of the real status of the Church's human side: it is capable of incarnating what is most terrible in the adversary by associating itself with his work of betraying God and humanity, of distortion, alienation, degradation, oppression, exploitation and death. But however deadly these manifestations of the Church and humanity may be, they cannot efface Christ's triumphant work that promises to the Church and to humanity the destiny of a glorious renewal, prefigured in Christ's resurrection. This renewal has already been commenced in the history of the world, is prefigured and proclaimed in all the movements of human renewal, cultural, artistic, social, economic and political. It is expressed partially in active, positive demands for recognition of human rights, social justice, economic development and political reconciliation, all intended to produce a dynamic, progressive humanity integrated into a worldwide community. The Holy Spirit gives to the receptive Church the liberty to participate in this renewal and to discern its source, the appropriate means to carry it out, and its final goal.

In this permanent and paradoxical combat for renewal, taking place between temporal forces animated by the renewing action of Christ and the adversary's powers of corruption, alienation and distortion, men are daily called to make choices that demand of them great spiritual discernment. They must be capable of subordinating their acts to Christ's acts by associating themselves with his struggle against the powers of destruction.

The dark pilgrim march   No guarantee other than that of Christ and his Holy Spirit can be given to assure them that

137

they are on the right side. They are all lonely pilgrims, each called to his own spiritual combat. Only Christ, the ultimate judge, can decide the issue by validating the obscure works he accepts. Each is responsible before the Lord for his own destiny, and no one can take his place in the decisive struggle of his humanity.

Where is the Church?   The Church is the place where these lonely pilgrims can meet and regroup. Its faithfulness encourages them, but its faithlessness discourages them. For the Church, as such, is no more assured than the individual of representing in temporal history the place where Christ triumphs over the world. As we have seen, it is itself susceptible to the forces of evil, which try to reduce its effectiveness in Christ's service.[1] There is in every Christian community a sitting Sanhedrin capable of condemning Christ to the cross. But there are also in it, at all times, courageous servants who make up the faithful Church. Christ accepts them, but only by the grace and virtue of his Spirit. Over against those Christians who have formed a coalition against their Lord's victory, they provide for the world a surety of his triumph and the sign of his victory. By their resistance to evil and often by their persecution, they prove to the Church and to all of humanity that Christ is the victor. They testify in the world and against the unfaithful Church what the authentic Church is all about. It is therefore of primary importance for the Church thus threatened to know that the only criterion of its existence and action is its conformity to Christ's work. Is it giving a true testimony in society of the Lord as he is known in his incarnation and historical abasement? Can one recognize in it the servant heir who has been disinherited in favor of the poor and oppressed, and who is yet humble enough to offer to the rich and powerful the testimony of their liberation? If so, it can be for humanity the sign promising liberation from all servitude and growth toward the one society, solidary and universal, prefiguring the Kingdom of God. But if such is not the case and if it becomes concerned for its own success, prestige and authority, for its own place in the world, if it conforms to the pressures exerted on it by the different groups possessing political, economic and social power who, in all political or economic systems, seek its support in order to consolidate their power, it thereby ceases to be the renewing leaven of societies, the salt that preserves them, and instead contributes to their degradation, to their dehumanization and finally to the destruction of the world. It bears an enormous responsibility for the destiny of the nations.

The unstable situation of the faithful Church in any society
The Church's fate here below is always tied in with that of the eternal Christ, the incarnate Christ, both suffering servant and triumphant Lord *(doulos* and *kyrios)*. According to circumstances, therefore, it can be called to endure the lot of the suffering servant rejected by the rich and powerful, or to enjoy the privileges of the sovereign Christ. But it is important that the privileges come as a result of faithfulness, not as a result of selfish conniving or cowardly compromise; the Church, like Babylon, the great prostitute, can be honored in the world.

The criterion of the Church's faithfulness in this specific area does not differ, then, from the criterion of its mysterious faithfulness to Christ, in a given time and place of history. It can trust no portrayals of itself other than that given to it by Christ. The stereotyped image of the Church as a scorned, rejected minority that exists only in the imagination of certain religious or political sects, who live on the margin of society more because of inhumanity than because of faithfulness to Christ, is just as false as the image of a triumphant Church, mistress and teacher of universal recognition, seated at the right hand of local political and economic authorities with whom she is supposed always to live in perfect harmony. The result of faithfulness is neither that of being in the majority and well established among reigning powers (because it is the titled representative of Christ the Lord, Christ Kyrios), nor necessarily that of being in the minority or persecuted (as though it were only the reflection of Christ the rejected servant, Christ Doulos).

In palaces and slums   One may never be certain that the Church that is in fact bearing witness to the real Christ in humanity is represented by an ecclesiastical institution or by the established Church. Nor is it necessarily in some desert hideout, fleeing from the world and apart from responsibility in humanity. The only guarantee that the Church is the real

Church is its faithfulness to the living Christ, and this can send it now into palaces, now into the streets, now into the deserts of poverty or the prisons of persecution, to the oppressed in their silent suffering or in their revolt. The Church is at home everywhere because Christ is at home everywhere. But the Church can also be rejected from any place because Christ can be rejected from any place. Moreover, the Church can be accepted or rejected in any place either because of its faithfulness or because of its unfaithfulness. Neither triumph nor social and political rejection is the sign of the Church's authenticity. For on all the levels of the social scale, on all planes of political, economic, cultural and social power, the Church can, in order to be well regarded, give in to the temptation to become a faithless prostitute Church; or it can be enlivened by the Holy Spirit and become a witnessing Church, conscious of its responsibility and its global mission for the development, peace and unity of mankind.

Truth first, not success   In all these areas the Church has serious decisions to make, forced upon it by historical situations. And these choices, though necessary, are always of a temporary nature, are always vitiated by their own precariousness, are always associated with the new steps the Church must make toward new choices that will bear witness anew to its conformity to the Lord. And it is only this desire to conform to the Lord's will that can make of it a power for the transformation of humanity. Its real effectiveness is never due to its success or lack of success, to its victories or its failures, to its prestige or the place it occupies in society.

A tragic optimism   The Church has good reason to be optimistic toward all this. But its optimism must be a tragic optimism,[2] an optimism that harbors no illusions about success and failure, but an optimism founded on the certainty of the promised final victory and on the faithfulness of the Lord. Through all situations and circumstances, no matter how serious the woes that strike the world, no matter how great the illusions born of a false hope, its desire to conform to the Lord's will enables the Church to maintain the active hope that motivates all its activities and undertakings with no consideration given to lack or presence of apparent success. By its faithfulness to its Lord it remains the most vigorous motivating force behind real progress and the authentic development of its true humanity.

Rejoicing in the coming of the Kingdom of God, its eyes fixed on the goal, far off yet near, of its history, the faithful Church will always be in the front ranks of society, ahead of its time, urgently proposing the reforms necessary for man's full development and effectively striving toward the goal of full human powers. Because it knows in whom it believes and where it is going, nothing can stop it in what it undertakes, even if the final result is not seen.

This is why the motto of William the Silent can well illustrate true realism, in this time of temporary political action, for every Christian and for all of humanity marching under the sign of a coming Kingdom. It is pure nonsense without faith, without a knowledge of the hidden destination of humanity, but it becomes a source of light and promise for all who, marching by faith like Abraham, hoping against hope,[3] forge ahead under the direction furnished for all creation by Christ himself: "It is not necessary to hope in order to undertake nor to succeed in order to persevere."

notes

PREFACE
[1] Cf. p. 15.

INTRODUCTION

[1] Paul VI, *Populorum progressio;* all quotations are from the official English translation as published in *The Pope Speaks,* 12 (1967), pp. 144-172.

[2] *World Development. The Challenge to the Churches;* published by the World Council of Churches; Geneva, 1968, 65 pp. We will quote this publication as "Beirut."

[3] *Uppsala Speaks, Section Reports of the Fourth Assembly of the World Council of Churches,* Uppsala, 1968; also published by the World Council of Churches; Geneva and New York, 1968, 97 pp. We will quote this publication as "Uppsala."

[4] We will also use one of the preparatory documents for the Uppsala Assembly, *God in Nature and History;* published by the World Council of Churches; Geneva, 1968, 31 pp. We will quote this publication as *"God in Nature. . . ."* The reader is also referred to the reports of the Conferences of the World Council of Churches at Montreal (1969) and Montreux (1970).

[5] This does not mean that these two kinds of knowledge are placed on the same plane. But since it is evident that they partially overlap, it is impossible fully to understand one without knowledge of the other, and vice versa. The historical mystery of the incarnation, alongside the problem for moderns of gaining knowledge of it, is a good example of overlapping. But overlapping does not mean confusion.

[6] Throughout this work we will use the word "Church" in its most general sense, including all Christians who confess Christ throughout the world or in any given place. And when we say "the Churches," we mean the collective Church divided into its various confessions. The term includes ecclesiastical institutions with no distinction made between hierarchical and nonhierarchical systems. We have left aside here the problem of ecclesiology.

[7] Cf. note 6 above.

[8] Although we have often quoted these texts word for word, we have made freer use of others. To learn the exact terms of these, the reader must consult the original documents. It was felt that frequent *verbatim* quotation would make the text far too heavy.

We have also felt it necessary to limit our references to the ecumenical documents mentioned above, in order to avoid discussing the many problems of methodology they raise — problems that have not been solved by any branch of scientific research, by any Church or by any theologian. For our present purposes, it will be sufficient to present the concrete solutions that have been provisionally proposed by laymen and theologians of all confessions.

CHAPTER I

[1] *God in Nature . . .*, pp. 7-8.
[2] Genesis 12:3. *God in Nature . . .*, p. 9.
[3] Genesis 1:26-30.
[4] Isaiah 6.
[5] Psalms 19, 29, 65, 67, 74, 75, 89, 96, 104, 136, 147, 148. *God in Nature . . .*, p. 10.
[6] Genesis 2:4b-25.
[7] *God in Nature . . .*, pp. 10-11.
[8] Isaiah 40:21f.; 42:5f.; 44:24f.; 45:12f.; 51:9f.
[9] John 1; Colossians 1; Hebrews 1.
[10] I Corinthians 15:44b-49.
[11] Uppsala, p. 61; cf. John 1:4; 11:25.
[12] *Populorum progressio*, p. 149.
[13] *Ibid.*
[14] The Word of God (the divine Logos) comes to us by the human word of those biblical witnesses who bear their testimony to it; and by modern interpretation of this testimony, to the extent that it is authenticated by the Holy Spirit.
[15] *God in Nature . . .*, pp. 16, 18-19. Genesis 2:7; 1 Corinthians 15:47. This does not exclude the fact that there is today an antagonism between the restored original state of man and his nature as changed by the ubiquitous effects of sin. Cf. Chapter II.
[16] Cf. pp. 49-50.
[17] John 5:17.
[18] In Chapter II we will study the necessity for the Holy Spirit to intervene in man's present state to enable him to make the proper response. The fact that his response does imply a break with the present world does not contradict what we have said.
[19] Beirut, p. 17.
[20] *Ibid.*
[21] *Ibid.*
[22] *Ibid.*
[23] *Populorum progressio*, p. 147.
[24] Ephesians 4:13.
[25] *Populorum progressio*, p. 149.
[26] Uppsala, p. 14.
[27] *Ibid.*, p. 52. The deliberate renouncement of economic prosperity and voluntary poverty preached by Christ, coupled with the curses he uttered against the rich, are so many protests against the tyranny of money and riches brought about by the corruption of sin (cf. Chapter II). They do not contradict, rather they confirm the divine

goal of harmonious economic growth for all, each person exercising proper control over his share (cf. pp. 64-65).

[28] Beirut, p. 18.

[29] *Ibid.*

[30] Genesis 1:28.

[31] *Populorum progressio,* p. 151.

[32] *Ibid.*

[33] *Gaudium et Spes,* no. 69, § 1; *Populorum progressio,* pp. 151-152.

[34] *Populorum progressio,* p. 152.

[35] Revelation 20-21.

[36] *God in Nature . . . ,* pp. 13-14.

[37] Genesis 1:26-28.

[38] *God in Nature . . . ,* p. 18.

[39] Beirut, p. 17.

[40] *Ibid.,* p. 19.

[41] *Populorum progressio,* p. 153.

[42] 2 Thessalonians 3:10.

[43] *Populorum progressio,* p. 153.

[44] *God in Nature . . . ,* pp. 16-17; *Populorum progressio,* pp. 153-154.

[45] *Populorum progressio,* p. 153.

[46] Seeing God at work in present development does not mean that everything within this development is in accord with God's plan. Rather the opposite is true. Cf. Chapter II.

[47] *Populorum progressio,* pp. 149, 153; *God in Nature . . . ,* pp. 15-16.

[48] Cf. Chapter II.

[49] *God in Nature . . . ,* p. 17; *Populorum progressio,* p. 155.

[50] *Populorum progressio,* p. 171.

[51] *Ibid.*

[52] Beirut, p. 15.

[53] *Ibid.,* pp. 15-16.

[54] Uppsala, p. 5; Beirut, p. 9.

[55] *Populorum progressio,* pp. 151-152. Cf. what we said about voluntary poverty, note 27 above.

[56] 1 John 3:17.

[57] *Populorum progressio,* p. 152.

[58] *Ibid.,* p. 156.

[59] *Ibid.*

[60] *Ibid.;* Beirut, pp. 30-31; Uppsala, pp. 50, 68.

[61] Beirut, pp. 17-18.

[62] Uppsala, pp. 61, 68.

[63] *God in Nature . . . ,* pp. 24-25.

[64] *Ibid.*

[65] Uppsala, p. 61.

[66] Cf. Chapter II B and Chapter III.

CHAPTER II

[1] *God in Nature . . . ,* pp. 17-18.

[2] *Populorum progressio,* p. 153.

3 *God in Nature . . . ,* p. 24.

4 *Populorum progressio,* p. 153.

5 *Ibid.,* p. 150.

6 Uppsala, p. 28.

7 *Populorum progressio,* p. 165.

8 *Ibid.,* p. 158.

9 *Ibid.*

10 No political, economic or social program can promise a harmonious life for men without a personal openness on their part to divine action. And no spiritual life can be lived out in faithfulness to God without a deliberate assumption of responsibility for man's temporal well-being within a general political project. Man can make no valid transformation of society without letting himself be transformed by divine action. And man cannot be transformed by God's action without participating in a general transformation of society. The question "Must man or society be transformed first?" is a false one. From the Christian point of view, the two go together.

11 *God in Nature . . . ,* pp. 23-24.

12 Uppsala, p. 28.

13 *Ibid.,* p. 45.

14 *Ibid.,* pp. 39-40.

15 *Populorum progressio,* p. 150.

16 *Ibid.,* p. 155.

17 *Ibid.,* pp. 152-153.

18 *Ibid.*

19 *Ibid.,* p. 151.

20 *Ibid.,* p. 159.

21 *Ibid.,* p. 155.

22 Uppsala, p. 45; Beirut, pp. 16-17.

23 Beirut, p. 19.

24 *Ibid.,* p. 16.

25 Luke 12:20; *Populorum progressio,* p. 160.

26 *Ibid.,* p. 154.

27 Uppsala, p. 48

28 *Populorum progressio,* p. 164.

29 *Ibid.,* pp. 164-165.

30 *Uppsala,* pp. 49-50.

31 *Ibid.,* pp. 65-66.

32 *Ibid.,* p. 69.

33 *Populorum progressio,* p. 164.

34 *Ibid.,* p. 150.

35 Beirut, p. 10.

36 *Populorum progressio,* p. 161.

37 Beirut, p. 9.

38 *Ibid.*

39 Uppsala, p. 5.

40 *Ibid.,* p. 45.

41 *Ibid.,* p. 5.

[42] Beirut, p. 17.

[43] 1 Corinthians 15:44b-49; Philippians 3:21; *God in Nature...*, pp. 13-14, 27-28.

[44] In using the term polemical to describe the make-up of the world, we are giving this adjective its etymological meaning. But this combat is one where God and those associated with him do not use the customary weapons of polemics, such as violence, lies, denigration, calumny, scorn for the adversary, etc.

[45] *God in Nature...*, p. 27.

[46] Uppsala, p. 28.

[47] Ephesians 4:13; 2 Corinthians 5:17; *Populorum progressio*, p. 153.

[48] John 5:17.

[49] 2 Corinthians 8:9. On this subject, see Chapter I, note 27.

[50] Uppsala, p. 61.

[51] *Ibid.*, p. 45.

[52] *Ibid.*, p. 28.

[53] *Ibid.*

[54] *Ibid.*

[55] *Ibid.*, p. 5.

[56] *Ibid.*, pp. 5-6.

[57] We do not intend to discuss here all the problems involved in this transformation, this conversion (*metanoia*) so amply discussed by the biblical authors. We will point out only some of its ethical aspects for individuals and societies.

[58] Uppsala, pp. 5-6.

[59] *Ibid.*, p. 5.

[60] *God in Nature...*, p. 27.

[61] Concerning the word polemical, see Chapter II, note 44.

[62] Uppsala, p. 45.

[63] *Ibid.*, p. 16.

[64] Since the work of Christ is visible only to the eyes of faith, that is, only to the minds of believers who make up the Church, it is generally considered to be the privileged place, or even the only place, where Christ's action takes place in the world. This focus on the Church has often kept the Church itself from discerning how Christ exercises his sovereignty over all of humanity. This is why, in most discussions today, Christ's action in the Church is privileged over the overall welfare of the world. The Church, however, is sent *into the world* to help men discover *what Christ is already doing for them* and to help them discover thereafter how to *be converted*, that is, how to conform more closely to what Christ has already begun in them, for them and by them. And for their neighbor. If Christ had to count only on the faithfulness of his Church to save the world, it would long ago have been plunged into complete annihilation. Ecumenical discussion over these last few decades has rediscovered the worldwide dimensions of Christ's kingship. That is why, following the example of Colossians 1, we speak of Christ's action in the world before speaking of the Church (to which Chapter III is devoted). The order itself is of little importance.

65 John 1:12; Beirut, p. 17.
66 *Ibid.*
67 Uppsala, p. 28.
68 *Ibid.*
69 *Populorum progressio,* p. 149.
70 *Ibid.,* p. 150.
71 Uppsala, p. 28. Cf. Ephesians 4:15 and 2 Peter 3:18.
72 Beirut, p. 17.
73 Uppsala, p. 6.
74 *Populorum progressio,* pp. 168-169.
75 Uppsala, p. 30; Beirut, p. 17.
76 Beirut, pp. 19-20.
77 1 Corinthians 13:12.
78 Matthew 22:30.
79 1 Corinthians 15:35f.
80 Uppsala, p. 61.
81 *Ibid.,* pp. 61, 28.
82 *Ibid.,* p. 13.
83 *Populorum progressio,* p. 149.
84 Uppsala, p. 65.
85 *Ibid.,* pp. 61-62.
86 *Ibid.,* pp. 14-15.
87 *God in Nature . . . ,* pp. 11, 27.
88 Matthew 21:33-39; Acts 7:1-53; Romans 7:7f.
89 Romans 5.
90 Galatians 4:3.
91 Acts 14:16; 17:30; Romans 3:25f.
92 2 Thessalonians 2 and Revelation; *God in Nature . . . ,* p. 12.
93 *Populorum progressio,* p. 67.
94 *Ibid.,* p. 149.
95 *Ibid.,* p. 158.
96 Uppsala, p. 38.
97 *Ibid.,* p. 14.
98 Beirut, pp. 18-19.
99 But, once again, not necessarily in the fashion in which it is taking place.
100 Beirut, pp. 18-19.
101 Uppsala, p. 29; *Populorum progressio,* p. 168.
102 Beirut, pp. 19-20.

CHAPTER III

1 Uppsala, p. 60.
2 *Ibid.,* p. 18.
3 Revelation 21. This is why the structure of the Church, the Body of Christ, is indicative of the structural solidarity of societies, both local and worldwide. The world has no definitive reality beyond that which is already signified in the Church, with which it will one day be fused. Christ is already at the head of this present double reality destined to become single. See Colossians 1.

[4] The "setting aside" that is the basis of holiness includes, as Christ's life and work show, both a break with the world and a new proximity among men, a new acceptance of responsibility toward them.

[5] Uppsala, p. 18. The participation in Christ's being (which the New Testament sums up by the expression "in Christ") is a communion that mobilizes all of man, with his intuition, will and reason. It entails a new ethical behavior that need not always be based on a complete socio-economic analysis. But this participation also puts his reason to work, and analysis is one of reason's chief tools.

[6] Uppsala, p. 28.

[7] *Ibid.*, p. 8.

[8] *Ibid.*, p. 11; *Populorum progressio,* p. 157.

[9] The Church in the totality of its members. Cf. note 6 of the Introduction.

[10] Uppsala, pp. 10, 14-15.

[11] *Ibid.*, pp. 4, 12-13.

[12] Beirut, p. 20.

[13] *Ibid.*, pp. 20, 44.

[14] Uppsala, p. 75.

[15] *Ibid.*, p. 16, § 16.

[16] *Ibid.*, p. 70.

[17] *Ibid.*, p. 13.

[18] *Ibid.*, p. 5.

[19] Romans 8:22.

[20] Uppsala, pp. 11-13.

[21] *Ibid.*, p. 15.

[22] Romans 12:1.

[23] Uppsala, pp. 13-14.

[24] *God in Nature . . . ,* p. 23.

[25] Uppsala, p. 29.

[26] *Ibid.*, pp. 30-31.

[27] *Ibid.*, p. 31.

[28] *Ibid.*, pp. 31-32. Cf. also the reports of the Conferences of the World Council of Churches at Montreal (1969) and Montreux (1970).

[29] Uppsala, p. 18.

[30] *Ibid.*, p. 6.

[31] *Ibid.*, p. 29.

[32] *Ibid.*, p. 18.

[33] *Ibid.*

[34] *Ibid.*, p. 12.

[35] Beirut, p. 19.

[36] *Ibid.*

[37] *Populorum progressio,* pp. 170-171.

[38] Beirut, p. 48.

[39] Uppsala, p. 45.

[40] *Ibid.*

[41] *Ibid.*, p. 61.

[42] Beirut, p. 19.

43 *Ibid.,* p. 20. On the subject of violence, see p. 170.

44 Uppsala, p. 16.

45 *Ibid.*

46 *Ibid.,* p. 15.

47 *Ibid.,* p. 17.

48 *Ibid.,* p. 28.

49 *Ibid.,* p. 30.

50 It must not be forgotten that by "Church" we are referring to the believers who make it up, in the world or in a given place, with no attempt to enter into a discussion of ecclesiology. Cf. note 6 of the Introduction.

51 Uppsala, p. 61.

52 *Ibid.,* p. 62.

53 *Ibid.,* p. 64.

54 *Ibid.,* p. 5.

55 *Ibid.,* p. 17.

56 *Ibid.,* p. 14.

57 *Ibid.*

58 *Ibid.,* pp. 14-15.

59 *Populorum progressio,* p. 161.

60 *Uppsala,* p. 46.

61 *Ibid.,* p. 62.

62 *Ibid.*

63 *Ibid.,* p. 66.

64 *Ibid.,* p. 32.

65 For example: the frequent, facile denunciation, in Western Churches, of atheism in communist countries and their silence toward the materialism of Western capitalism based on the almost exclusive priority of profit in creative activity; and the exactly inverse attitude of certain Eastern Churches.

66 Uppsala, p. 45.

67 *Ibid.,* p. 45.

68 *Beirut,* p. 9.

69 The Church's overall responsibility and its responsibility for a given nation must not be considered a function of its numerical strength, its majority or minority position in a society or the audience it enjoys. Its purpose should not be to seek a Christian regime to ensure its success and legitimize its interventions in society. Rather it is to do and say what it has to do and say without worrying excessively about whether it is well received or not. Results — which are to be sought after — must never become the first criterion of its faithfulness.

70 Uppsala, p. 51.

71 *Ibid.*

72 *Ibid.,* p. 33.

73 *Ibid.,* p. 69. "Regional" is used more and more frequently to designate a multi-national area, halfway between the nation and the world (e.g., Europe).

74 Revelation 21:5.

[75] 2 Corinthians 5:17.
[76] Uppsala, p. 60.
[77] *Ibid.*, pp. 60-61.
[78] *Ibid.*, p. 45.
[79] Beirut, pp. 16-17.
[80] *Ibid.*, p. 17.
[81] *Populorum progressio*, p. 165.
[82] 1 John 3:2f.
[83] 1 Corinthians 15:44b-49.
[84] *God in Nature . . .*, pp. 13-14.
[85] 2 Thessalonians 2 and Revelation.
[86] Acts 14:16; 17:30; Romans 3:25f.
[87] *God in Nature . . .*, p. 12.
[88] Romans 8:18-25.
[89] Revelation 21:4; 1 Corinthians 15:47.
[90] *God in Nature . . .*, p. 20.
[91] Uppsala, p. 28.
[92] *Ibid.*, p. 6.
[93] *Ibid.*, p. 5.
[94] *Populorum progressio*, p. 170.
[95] Beirut, pp. 20-21.
[96] Uppsala, p. 18.
[97] *God in Nature . . .*, pp. 25-26.

CHAPTER IV

[1] The belief in one force ruling the world of politics and economics, leading them finally to death, while Christ rules only over the new world of the Church, is a dualistic, Manichean belief that inevitably leads to a double morality. The believer is thus divided into two persons obeying different laws depending on whether he is operating in the private domain or in the collective circles of society. Of course, even in our conception relationships between individual Christians are on an ethical level different from the collective relationships of social groups, but there is neither discontinuity nor a breakdown of ethics between the different levels.

[2] Here we are referring only to the human side of Good Friday, where may be seen man's deep revolt against God and his radical capacity for evil. And we are saying that man's tragic propensity toward evil is temporary. But the work the crucified Christ accomplished for the world, an expression of divine love and promise of pardon for humanity, is eternally valid.

[3] Hebrews 12-13.

[4] Philippians 3:20.

[5] Only by virtue of Christ's action; without it, every society is liable to the radical judgment of God.

[6] Hebrews 13:14.

[7] 1 Corinthians 3:11-15; 4:5. *God in Nature . . .*, pp. 15, 21, 25, 29-31.

[8] Uppsala, p. 18.

[9] Romans 8:21.

10 Romans 8:37-39; 1 Corinthians 13:12.

11 Romans 12:2.

12 The Old and New Testaments provide examples of historical attempts at temporal establishments based on the laws of this Kingdom, in specific cultures, emphasizing different aspects of each example. Working from these historical examples and comparing them with present situations, we may discover how Christ works in the world today and may, all the while imploring the Holy Spirit's continual intervention, propose new models capable of expressing certain aspects of his will for new cultures and new conditions.

13 Uppsala, p. 62.

14 *Gaudium et Spes,* No. 4, par. 1; *Populorum progressio,* p. 149.

15 Let us recall that the triumph of Easter has nothing mechanical or automatic about it. It is always dependent on the mystery of God's free decision and his election and must remain so through the final judgment. Cf. Chapters II and III.

16 Uppsala, p. 62.

17 *Ibid.; Populorum progressio,* p. 149.

18 Uppsala, p. 62.

19 In spite of the care he took to maintain his distance from the Zealots whose goals were only political, it seems that he was condemned as a Zealot.

20 *Populorum progressio,* pp. 148-149.

21 Uppsala, p. 29.

22 *Ibid.,* p. 68; *Populorum progressio,* pp. 170-171.

23 Matthew 25:31-40.

24 Even more detailed are the directives proposed by the report of the World Conference on Church and Society held in 1966 under the auspices of the World Council of Churches, and the reports of the conferences held in Montreal (1969) and Montreux (1970). These reports may be obtained from the World Council of Churches, Publications Service, 475 Riverside Drive, New York, N. Y. 10027, or from the Geneva office: 150 route de Ferney, CH-1211, Geneva 20, Switzerland.

25 Beirut, p. 15.

26 *Ibid.,* p. 20.

27 *Ibid.,* p. 19.

28 *Ibid.,* p. 22.

29 Beirut, p. 43.

30 *Ibid.,* pp. 27-41.

31 *Ibid.,* pp. 27-28.

32 Uppsala, p. 31.

33 Beirut, p. 20.

34 Uppsala, pp. 39-40, 48.

35 *Ibid.,* pp. 64, 67, 68-69, 72.

36 *Ibid.,* p. 18.

37 *Ibid.,* p. 69; cf. Chapter III, note 73.

38 *Ibid.*

39 *Ibid.*

[40] Beirut, pp. 42-43.
[41] *Populorum progressio,* p. 161; Beirut, p. 9.
[42] Beirut, pp. 12-13, 25, 37.
[43] *Populorum progressio,* p. 161.
[44] Uppsala, p. 63.
[45] *Ibid.,* p. 64.
[46] *Ibid.,* p. 68; *Populorum progressio,* p. 161.
[47] Uppsala, p. 70.
[48] *Populorum progressio,* p. 169.
[49] Beirut, p. 49.
[50] *Ibid.*
[51] Uppsala, p. 71.
[52] *Ibid.,* p. 51.
[53] *Ibid.,* pp. 68-69.
[54] *Ibid.,* p. 29; Ephesians 4:12.
[55] *Ibid.*
[56] *Ibid.,* p. 33.

CONCLUSION

[1] Cf. Luke 22:31.
[2] The expression is E. Mounier's.
[3] Romans 4:18.